Ancient Northumberland

By Clive Waddington and Dave Passmore

First published 2004
© CountryStore (an imprint of The Design Desk)

ISBN 0-9530163-6-6

Photographic contributions are from Peter Forrester, Aron Mazel, Tim Gates, the authors or as shown. Cover picture by Peter Forrester.
Illustrations by Ben Johnson.

CountryStore, Milfield, Wooler, Northumberland, NE71 6JD
www.thedesigndesk.co.uk   Email: books@thedesigndesk.co.uk

The funding for producing this book has been provided by the Aggregates Levy Sustainability Fund through Defra and English Heritage.

Contents

List of Illustrations

Acknowledgements

This book draws on years of work carried out by many archaeologists who have studied the prehistory of Northumberland. In particular we would like to acknowledge the work of Stan Beckensall, Colin Burgess, Tim Gates, Anthony Harding, George Jobey, Roger Miket, Chris Tolan-Smith, Peter Topping, Rob Young, the Northumberland National Park Authority, the Northumberland Archaeological Group and the Society of Antiquaries of Newcastle-upon-Tyne. All have made a significant contribution to understanding the prehistory of the region and to them all we owe a debt of thanks. Many others, too numerous to mention here, have also made important contributions to the prehistoric archaeology and environmental history of the region and their work is happily acknowledged too.

In recent years English Heritage have greatly enabled research in the region, as has the Northumberland National Park Authority (NNPA) and Paul Frodsham from the NNPA deserves special mention. The funding for producing this book has been provided by the Aggregates Levy Sustainability Fund through Defra and English Heritage. Lyndsay Allason-Jones has kindly allowed us to photograph many of the fine artefacts in the Museum of Antiquities display and to publish some archive pictures. Tim Gates has also allowed us to reproduce a number of his fine aerial photographs and Nick Hodgson has provided the photograph of the South Shields roundhouse.

The views expressed in this book are those of the authors and do not necessarily reflect the views of those whose work is cited. Finally, we would like to thank Colm O'Brien and Jonathan Last for their invaluable comments on previous drafts of the text which has improved the book considerably. Any errors or omissions remain, of course, our own.

Preface

Northumberland is an extraordinary place; a land of stunning scenery and world-famous archaeological heritage on the one hand, yet a gentle and rolling landscape with little-known archaeological gems on the other. Although best known for Hadrian's Wall and the unparalleled romance of its many castles, the county is also home to the finest examples of prehistoric rock art in England, the greatest concentration of henge monuments, the largest number of hillforts and defended sites, and one of the best preserved Bronze Age upland landscapes in Europe in the form of the Cheviot Hills. Although not always as visible as the more famous sites, these prehistoric remains are just as important and have equally interesting tales to tell. This book is dedicated to sharing what is known about the early inhabitants of the region; their way of life, their homes and monuments, and their relationship with the land. We have gained much from our research in the county, having both worked here for over a decade. We have endeavoured to undertake a complementary and integrated approach to our research; one as an archaeologist who dabbles in the palaeoenvironment, the other as a palaeoenvironmentalist who dabbles in archaeology. The result, we hope, is that our understanding of the prehistory of the region has moved on and that we are in a better position to ask new questions. At the same time we hope to make this story of the region's past accessible to a wider audience.

CW and DP
August 2003

1   Prehistory in Northumberland

Prehistory is the name given to the period of time before written records began, which, in Britain, means all human activity prior to the arrival of the Romans in 43 AD. Given this lack of written sources, prehistorians have to rely exclusively on physical remains to understand the past. All physical things created, used and named by people are referred to as 'material culture' and this is the stuff of archaeology. It includes the artefacts and structures that we are familiar with, such as stone tools, bronze weapons, roundhouse platforms and hillforts. It also includes natural objects and places that have been altered and named by people, such as engraved rocks, caves and springs.

Prehistorians, moreover, also consider the environment and how this has changed through time, as such studies can reveal evidence for how people have adapted to, or modified, the landscape. For example, they can reveal when people cleared trees in order to farm the land, the types of crops that were grown, and why people may have lived in one area and not another. It is this combining of various strands of evidence that allows the prehistorian to put together the jigsaw puzzle of the past. With advances in modern scientific techniques, the prehistorian is assisted by diverse specialist input that includes, amongst others, DNA and faunal analyses, pollen analysis, aerial photography and dating techniques. The prehistorian is, therefore, an integrator who brings together a wide range of information to reconstruct the past.

"Working on the Edge"

As archaeologists dealing with prehistory have to assimilate data from disparate disciplines they often find themselves working on the edge - at the boundaries between different subject areas. Although this can be challenging, it allows the prehistorian to approach the past from a wider and more holistic perspective, thus holding in check the obsessive tendencies that so often accompany specialist subjects.

I Archaeologists excavating pottery from a Neolithic pit, north of Milfield village.

2 Excavations at Howick on a cliff edge

The notion of 'working on the edge' also extends to the physical situations that archaeologists find themselves in from time to time. As archaeological sites are usually better preserved in remote places, where there has been less modern development, fieldwork often takes place in marginal areas on the edge of our settled landscape. Recent examples in Northumberland include excavations on a cliff edge at Howick and on a Cheviot hilltop at Wether Hill.

Archaeology has become increasingly popular over the last decade, partly as a result of a burgeoning media interest, and partly because people have an increasing interest in their heritage and how it defines their own identity. Archaeological and historical documentaries are featured on television virtually every day of the week and some satellite channels such as 'Discovery Channel' are almost entirely given over to them. Regular archaeological pieces appear in the national newspapers and on radio, and

3 The author Clive Waddington filming with the BBC at Howick

important discoveries get reported on the national news. Northumberland has attracted its share of popular interest in recent years with two 'Meet the Ancestors' programmes (on Bamburgh and Howick) and two 'Time Team' editions (on Holy Island and Birdoswald on the Roman Wall, though the latter lies just inside Cumbria). In addition, attendances at local history and archaeology societies remain buoyant, and we have lost count of the number of packed village halls where we have been invited to talk about archaeology. It has become essential that archaeologists engage with this popular interest and open up their work to a wider public audience. After all, the main purpose of archaeology is to provide society with a sense of its past. The consequence of this is that it should add to people's quality of life, sense of identity and understanding of both the past and present. Building on these sentiments, this book is intended as a celebration of Northumbrian culture and landscape; one that aims to provide an overview of its prehistoric past.

Northumberland is one of the largest counties in England, covering an area of just under 2000 square miles. It is a landscape characterised by great variation, boasting the domed peaks of the Cheviot massif, the heather moorlands of the sandstone escarpments, fertile river valleys and lowland basins, the coastal plain and a magnificent, yet varied, coastline. However, the area of land covered by the modern county was not a discrete entity in prehistory. The prehistoric archaeology north of the Tweed, in what is modern-day south-east Scotland, shows little difference to the cultural remains south of the Tweed, and therefore what we now think of as 'Northumberland' was rather a heartland

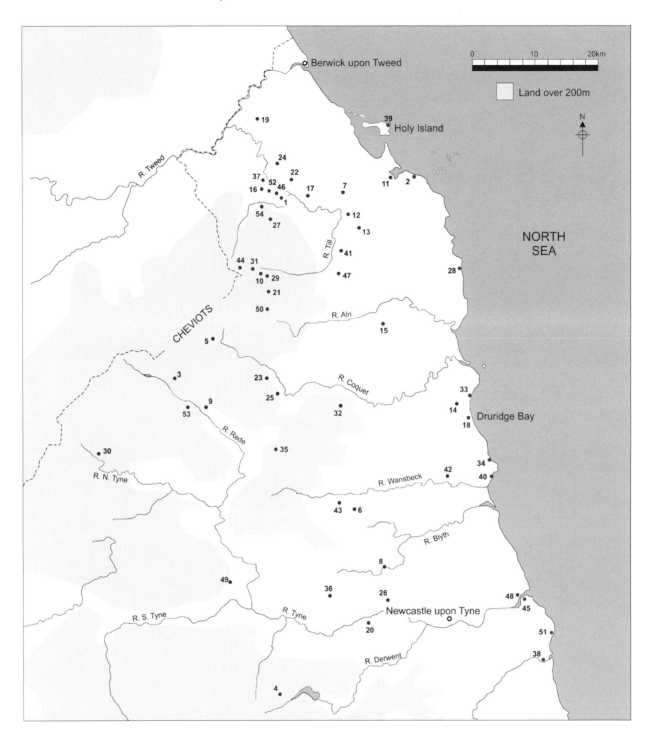

1 Akeld Steads, 2 Bamburgh, 3 Bellshiel, 4 Birkside Fell, 5 Black Stitchell Rigg, 6 Bolam Lake, 7 Bowden Doors,
8 Braid Hill, 9 Brigantium, 10 Brough Law, 11 Budle Bay, 12 Chatton Park Hill, 13 Chatton Sandyford Moor,
14 Chevington, 15 Corby's Crags, 16 Coupland, 17 Dod Law, 18 Druridge Bay, 19 Duddo Stone Circle,
20 Eltringham Farm, 21 Fawdon Dene, 22 Fenton Hill, 23 Five Barrows, Holystone, 24 Goatscrag, 25 Harehaugh,
26, Heddon-on-the-Wall, 27 Houseledge West, 28 Howick, 29 Ingram Hill, 30 Kennel Hall Knowe,
31 Linhope Burn, 32 Lordenshaws, 33 Low Hauxley, 34 Lyne Hill, 35 Manside Cross, Elsdon,
36 Matfen Standing Stone, 37 Milfield, 38 Monkwearmouth, 39 Ness End, 40 Newbiggin by the Sea,
41 Old Bewick, 42 Pegswood, 43 Poind and his Man, 44 Standrop Rigg, 45 South Shields, 46 Thirlings,
47 Titlington, 48 Wallsend, 49 Warden Hill, 50 Wether Hill, 51 Whitburn, 52 Woodbridge Farm,
53 Woolaw, 55 Yeavering

4 Map of Northumberland showing sites mentioned in the text

within a wider region. This is not to say that this area did not have a defined boundary at certain periods, but rather that its modern extent does not necessarily reflect the territories of the past. Today, Northumberland is defined on two sides by major river valleys: the Tweed and its tributaries to the north and the Tyne and its tributaries to the south. To the west Northumberland extends over much of, but not beyond, the Cheviot Hills, while to the east it is bounded by the coast. Throughout this book we will focus on the modern geographic entity that constitutes Northumberland, but we will refer to the archaeology of adjoining regions where appropriate in order to emphasise themes that apply just as well to Northumberland.

Most of Northumberland's rivers flow from west to east, tracing a course through lush, deeply incised valleys. The only exceptions are the river Till (known as the Breamish in its upper reach) which flows northwards into the Tweed, and the North and South Tynes which flow south and north respectively until they combine at Warden at the aptly named 'Watersmeet'. Understanding the geography of Northumberland is one of the keys to unlocking the prehistoric settlement pattern of the area, and it is perhaps no coincidence that the modern settlement pattern is largely focused around valley-based communities. Northumberland's long-standing fishing tradition no doubt echoes back to the first settlers in the region who would have found the coast a plentiful resource. Remains dating from all prehistoric periods have been found along the coastal margin, testifying to its particular attraction for successive groups of early inhabitants.

The population of Northumberland (not including the conurbation of Tyne and Wear) is today 300,000 people, with more than half residing in the industrial towns in the south-east of the county. It is the most sparsely populated of all English counties but, as we shall see, this was not the case in the Bronze and Iron Ages when some areas were more thickly populated than now. Throughout prehistory the population of Northumberland will have varied considerably, from the time of the first hunter-gatherer groups to the time of widespread Bronze Age farms. Estimating actual population sizes is a tricky business, and not particularly reliable, but a relative sense of population can be acquired by observing the number and distribution of surviving settlements. On this basis it is astonishing to think that many of the valleys, particularly in the uplands, were much more heavily populated in the later Bronze Age and Iron Age than they are today. More people were required to work the land and more land was in agricultural production than today.

Therefore, it is necessary to shed our 21st century concepts of the Northumberland landscape we know if we are to understand what this land looked like, and how it was thought about, by prehistoric peoples.

Further Reading

General works dealing with the prehistory of Northumberland include the following:

Beckensall, S. 2003. *Prehistoric Northumberland*. Stroud: Tempus.

Burgess, C.B. 1984. The Prehistoric Settlement of Northumberland: A Speculative Survey. In R. Miket and C. Burgess (eds.) *Between And Beyond The Walls: Essays on the Prehistory and History of North Britain in Honour of George Jobey*. Edinburgh: John Donald: 126-175.

Higham, N. 1986. *The Northern Counties to AD1000*. Harlow: Longman.

Huntley, J. P. and S. M. Stallibrass 1995. *Plant and Vertebrate Remains From Archaeological Sites in Northern England: Data Reviews and Future Directions*. Durham: Architectural and Archaeological Society of Northumberland and Durham.

Waddington, C. 1999. *A Landscape Archaeological Study of the Mesolithic-Neolithic in the Milfield Basin, Northumberland*. Oxford: British Archaeological Reports, British Series 291.

Waddington, C. 1999. *Land of Legend. Discovering Ancient Northumberland*. Wooler: Country Store Publishing.

5 The Cheviot landscape from summit of Cheviot

2 Environment

Geological history

The origins of the Northumberland landscape can be traced back 430 million years when sedimentary rocks were formed in the shallow seas of what is now the extreme north-west part of the region. Around 345-410 million years ago volcanic activity gave rise to a new era of landscape formation. This period of 'volcanism' witnessed the deposition of ashes, lavas and agglomerates in north-west Northumberland with granite plugs forming the final phase of local rock formation. This complex of volcanic or 'igneous' rocks today forms the rounded domes of the Cheviot range, characterised by their steep sides, round tops and interlocking valleys. The tallest of the Cheviot Hills is the 'Cheviot' itself which reaches a maximum height of 815m.

"Ice wastes to green land"

To the south-west the landscape is dominated by the uplands of the Northern Pennine massif. Reaching a maximum elevation of 893m at Cross Fell, near Alston, these hills are predominantly formed of limestones and sandstones that were laid down in warm, shallow seas and river valleys some 280-345 million years ago during the geological period known as the 'Carboniferous'. Sandstones, limestones, cementstones, shales and coal measures of similar age and origin also underlie much of the central and eastern part of the county to the north of the River Tyne.

6 View across the South Tyne valley - a typical north Pennine dale

7 Hadrian's Wall following an outcrop of the Whin Sill

Towards the end of the Carboniferous period, about 290 million years ago, the sedimentary rocks of north-east England were intruded by molten rock from within the earth's crust which cooled to form layers of hard dolerite that are highly resistant to erosion. Known as the Great Whin Sill complex, this intrusion forms long ridges of dolerite that are orientated broadly south-west to north-east across central and eastern Northumberland. They are most spectacularly exposed in the valley of the South Tyne where they form a prominent cliff edge that is followed by Hadrian's Wall, although there are also large exposures at the coast where the rock outcrops, such as Howick Scar south of Craster.

The distribution and configuration of these geological formations has been much affected by millions of years of earth movements along major regional fault lines and the actions of rivers, sea and wind, so that by about 2 million years ago the upland and lowland contrasts in the Northumbrian landscape were well-established. On the south-east and eastern flanks of the Cheviots the landscape owes much to geological differences in the Carboniferous rocks. Here, broad vales underlain by relatively soft cementstones are overlooked by west-facing craggy ridges formed by Fell Sandstones. These coarse-grained sandstones form two parallel escarpments that curve around the Cheviot block with their more gentle 'dip' slopes falling away towards the coast. The Fell Sandstone is a warm buff colour when cut and has been used around much of the county to build farms, cottages and castle walls. This hardy rock is relatively resistant to erosion, although it can be formed into a variety of strange shapes by the action of water and wind. Some of the county's finest waterfalls can be found in the streams that tumble off the sandstone fells.

8 A Mesolithic rock shelter at Goatscrag on the sandstone escarpment

Over much of the eastern part of the county the Carboniferous sedimentary formations dip gently towards the North Sea, giving a relatively low and often flat coastal plain that separates the uplands from the present coast. The coast itself has a varied topography that reflects the complex geology and long history of coastal erosion and sediment deposition. Between Berwick-on-Tweed and Alnmouth the coastline features numerous sandy bays and rugged headlands. Here, elevated outcrops of the Whin Sill form the offshore Farne Islands and upstanding coastal promontories on which the castles of Bamburgh and Dunstanburgh are located. To the south of Alnmouth the coast and inland plain has been extensively modified by human settlement and industrial activity, particularly as a result of opencast and deep shaft mining of Carboniferous coal formations. Headlands and bays occur along this stretch of coast, with Druridge Bay, the longest sandy bay in the county, bounded by sandstone promontories at its northern and southern limits.

9 View over the coastal plain to the Farne Islands

Ice Age Northumberland

Over the past 2 million years, the regional landscape was further modified during a period of dramatic climate change known by geologists as the 'Quaternary' period. The Quaternary is characterised by a see-sawing of the earth's climate between cold glaciations (commonly called the 'Ice Ages') and warm interglacial periods with climates similar to those of the present day. Quaternary scientists believe that Northumberland was covered by glacial ice on at least two occasions, most recently some 18,000 years ago during the last major glacial period (in Britain termed the 'Devensian'). At the peak of this glaciation higher parts of the Northumberland landscape in the Northern Pennines and Cheviot Hills probably supported local ice caps, but elsewhere in the county the landscape was overrun by ice sheets originating in the Scottish Highlands, the Lake District and the Southern Uplands of Scotland. The Devensian glaciation accomplished considerable erosion of upland parts of Northumberland, particularly in the main valleys of the Cheviots and Northern Pennines, although these valleys lack the spectacular over-deepened glacial troughs that are characteristic of the nearby Lake District.

Beyond the high upland valleys, lower parts of the landscape were covered with varying thicknesses of sediment composed of material eroded and transported by the ice sheets. This material was laid down both during, and shortly after, glaciation. Ice sheets flowing east and south across the coastal plain deposited sequences of till (comprising boulders and gravel mixed with sand, silt and clay) that often exceed 6m in thickness. In several localities along the coast, for example at Whitley Bay, these sediments infill river valleys formed during earlier times.

10 The Bizzel - a glaciated valley in the Cheviot Hills

De-glaciation of the region, which probably left the region ice-free by around 15,000 years ago, released vast quantities of meltwater that also had an important role in shaping the landscape. In some localities meltwater torrents beneath, and adjacent to, glacial ice have cut deep

11 A glacial meltwater channel on Whitfield Moor near Alston

channels on hilltops and valley sides, and many examples survive today as dry valleys in the high ground of the Northern Pennines and Cheviots.

In other areas, sediment-laden meltwaters deposited thick sequences of sand and gravel outwash terraces. These landscapes are particularly well-preserved as distinctive hummocky terrain in the South Tyne valley between Hexham and Haltwhistle, and on the eastern flanks of the Cheviots between Powburn and Milfield.

12 Sand and gravel outwash deposits in the South Tyne valley near Haydon Bridge

Post-Glacial Environmental Change

Global warming at the end of the Devensian glaciation marked the beginning of the current interglacial period, known as the 'Holocene', which spans the past 12,000 years of the earth's history. Landscape modifications during this period of relatively warm temperatures have been minor by comparison with the effects of glaciation, but have nevertheless contributed much to the character of the Northumbrian landscape. Significant environmental changes have occurred through sea-level changes along the coastal margins, while inland the valley floors of the region have been much altered by repeated episodes of river flooding. The most extensive modifications of the landscape, however, have been driven by the combined effects of post-glacial climate change and human impact on the region's vegetation and soil cover.

The Coast

The Northumberland coast has witnessed major landscape changes as a result of post-glacial sea-level rise. At the beginning of the Holocene, sea levels were some 30m below the present level, and the modern coastal margin of the county looked east over a vast low-lying tidal plain that formed part of the land bridge connecting eastern England to the north-west European mainland. This landscape was gradually drowned by sea-level rise, so that by around 6000 years ago the Northumberland coast was more or less established in its present location. Wind, waves and tides have further modified the region's coastal landscape. In many places the coast has been retreating as the sea has undermined cliff faces, a process that continues to threaten coastal towns (for example at

14 An exposed peat bed at Low Hauxley. This dark layer represents an ancient land surface dating back as far as the Neolithic

Amble), agricultural land and archaeological sites (such as the Mesolithic house site at Howick). Elsewhere, extensive parts of the coast have been prone to accumulation of blown sand; indeed sandy beaches and dunes were once virtually continuous along the Northumberland coast. In the south-eastern part of the county, however, these environments have been greatly disturbed by recent human activity. Sandy beaches and dunefields are best developed in sheltered bays such as those adjacent to Holy Island and between Bamburgh and Seahouses, while several localities have accumulated dunefields up to several metres thick that bury former coastal landscapes. The latter can be seen at Low Hauxley and Druridge Bay where peats, tree stumps and ancient lagoons lie buried beneath sand dunes.

River Valleys

Inland from the coast the most significant landform changes during post-glacial times have occurred in the region's valley floors as a result of river erosion and the deposition of sediments. Erosion has been most prevalent in steeper upland valleys and here river channels have cut deep into their valley floors leaving earlier floodplains abandoned as flights of river terraces. River channels in these environments are prone to shifting their course across the valley floor and terrace surfaces often exhibit sinuous depressions that represent former watercourses. The gentler gradients of lowland valleys and alluvial basins, by contrast, have tended to promote the deposition of sediment. In these valley settings the floodplains of early Holocene times may be buried beneath several metres of alluvium.

Forests, Bogs and Human Activity

By far the most widespread and dramatic landscape changes, however, have concerned the region's vegetation cover. The disappearance of ice cover, around 15,000 years ago, revealed a barren, inhospitable landscape of bare ground largely devoid of vegetation or soil cover. Pioneer 'tundra' vegetation, including lichens, grasses and dwarf shrubs, was quickly established during this climatic transition, and during the period between 12-11,000 years ago conditions were sufficiently warm to allow the spread of juniper and alpine heath with local stands of birch trees. However, a return to cold, dry conditions about 11,000 years ago forced a reversion to barren, open landscapes with tundra vegetation. A further thousand or so years passed before rapid climate warming established the beginning of the Holocene interglacial and a more hospitable and varied habitat for plants, animals and humans.

During the early Holocene, between 10,000-7000 years ago, mixed deciduous woodland expanded across most of the Northumberland landscape. Early forests largely comprised birch, hazel and pine, but by around 7000 years ago the combination of mature soil development and slightly warmer temperatures than those of today had allowed dense forests of oak and elm to develop in the well-drained lowland and upland areas with deeper soils. By the middle part of the Holocene, between 7000-5000 years ago, Britain's climate had entered a period of sustained warmth, with mean air temperatures some 2-4°C higher than those of today. However, this warmth was associated with more oceanic conditions, and hence an increase in rainfall. On the cooler, exposed

15 River terrace environment with abandoned river channel at Featherstone in the South Tyne valley

hilltops of the region the wetter climate combined with acid soils to promote bog formation. The impact of increased rainfall was lessened over much of Northumberland due to the rain-shadow effect of the Northern Pennines and Cheviot Hills, but rising water tables nevertheless favoured the spread of alder-dominated woodland and fen-carr in areas of poorly drained soils, particularly in upland localities and low-lying valley and floodplain wetlands.

Extensive, early-mid Holocene virgin forest cover across the region was host to a rich variety of plant, animal and birdlife, and occasional small clearings in the forest cover (created by natural and man-made fires) provided campsites and hunting grounds for groups of hunter-gatherer-fisherfolk. Forest regeneration in small clearings gave rise to more open woodland with understorey trees and shrubs that included ash, birch and hazel. In general, however, these early disturbance episodes are unlikely to have made a significant impact on the Northumberland forest cover, except perhaps in marginal areas where localised bog, heath and moorland patches were established.

Mid-Holocene times, between 6000-2000 years ago, witnessed a gradual increase in woodland clearance as people began to domesticate animals and grow cereal crops such as wheat and barley. This activity is likely to have been most intensive on well-drained valley sides and floors in the vicinity of larger settlement areas. However, woodland clearance appears to have been localised and often temporary and it was not until the later Iron Age and the arrival of the Romans in the early part of the 1st millennium AD that major and permanent deforestation began to take place. Today we have become accustomed to a largely agricultural landscape that has persisted since the last major clearances of the late Medieval period, and it bears witness to the scale and longevity of the impact of humans on the natural vegetation of Northumberland. It is perhaps ironic that only the modern conifer plantations of Kielder Forest can begin to provide some impression of the vast expanse of natural forest cover that was once so characteristic of the Northumberland landscape.

16 The Kielder Forest landscape in the upper reaches of the North Tyne valley

Further Reading

General
Lowe, J.J. and Walker, M.J.C. 1997. *Reconstructing Quaternary Environments.* London: Longman.
Roberts, N. 1998. *The Holocene: An Environmental History.* Oxford: Blackwell.
Simmons, I. G. 1996. *The Environmental Impact of Later Mesolithic Cultures.* Edinburgh: Edinburgh University Press.

Northumberland
Archer, D. 1992. *Land of Singing Waters. Rivers and Great Floods of Northumbria.* Stocksfield, Northumberland: Spredden Press.
Bridgland, D.R., Horton, B.P. and Innes, J.B. (eds). 1999. *The Quaternary of North-East England; Field Guide.* London: Quaternary Research Association.
Clapperton, C. M. 1971. The pattern of deglaciation in north Northumberland. *The Institute of British Geographers Transactions* 53: 67-78.
Davies, G. and Turner, J. 1979. Pollen Diagrams from Northumberland. *New Phytologist* 82: 783-804.
Dumayne, L. and Barber, K.E. 1994. The impact of the Romans on the environment of northern England: pollen data from three sites close to Hadrian's Wall. *The Holocene* 4: 165-173.
Higham, N. 1986. *The Northern Counties to AD1000.* London: Longman.
Macklin, M. G., D. G. Passmore and B.T. Rumsby. 1992. Climatic and cultural signals in Holocene alluvial sequences: the Tyne basin, northern England. In S. Needham and M. Macklin. (eds.) *Alluvial Archaeology in Britain.* Oxford: Oxbow: 123-139.
Moores, A., D. Passmore and A. Stevenson. 1999. High resolution palaeochannel records of Holocene valley floor environments in the North Tyne basin, northern England. In A. G. Brown and T. Quine (eds.) *Fluvial Processes and Environmental Change.* London, John Wiley: 283-310.
Passmore, D. G., M. G. Macklin, *et al*. 1992. A Holocene alluvial sequence in the lower Tyne valley, northern Britain: A record of river response to environmental change. *The Holocene* 2(2): 138-47.
Passmore, D.G. and Macklin, M.G. 2000. Late Holocene floodplain and channel development in a wandering gravel-bed river: The River South Tyne at Lambley, northern England. *Earth Surface Processes and Landforms*, 25: 1237-1256.
Plater, A. J. and Shennan, I. 1992. Evidence of Holocene sea-level change from the Northumberland coast, eastern England. *Proceedings of the Geologists' Association*, 103: 201-16.
Robson, D.A. 1965. *A guide to the geology of Northumberland and the Borders.* Transactions of the Natural History Society of Northumberland, Durham and Newcastle upon Tyne 1: 77.
Robson, D.A. (ed). 1980. *The Geology of North East England.* Newcastle upon Tyne: Hancock Museum.
Simmons, I.G. and Innes, J.B. 1987. Mid-Holocene adaptations and later Mesolithic forest disturbance in Northern England. *Journal of Archaeological Science*, 14: 385-403.
Tipping, R. 1996. The Neolithic Landscapes of the Cheviot Hills and Hinterland: Palaeoenvironmental Research. *Northern Archaeology*, 13/14: 17-33.
Tipping, R. 1998. The chronology of Late Quaternary fluvial activity in part of the Milfield Basin, north east England. *Earth Surface Processes and Landforms* 23 (9): 845-855.

3 Palaeolithic and Mesolithic

Palaeolithic

The term Palaeolithic means 'Old Stone Age' and refers to all periods of hominid existence before the end of the last Ice Age. It is divided into Lower, Middle and Upper periods with anatomically modern humans, like us, only appearing in north-west Europe at the start of the Upper Palaeolithic, around 40,000 years ago. There are no definite remains earlier than the latter part of the Upper Palaeolithic period (*c.*15,000 BC) in Northumberland, although there have been accounts of much older, Lower Palaeolithic hand-axes being found. However, such finds may have been introduced to the region as a result of ballast dumping along the coast, or from flint collectors who brought examples back to the north-east from elsewhere.

"Hunter-gatherers and fisherfolk"

The presence of humans in the north-east during the late Upper Palaeolithic period is suggested by a flint blade found on Eltringham Farm near Prudhoe and an important assemblage of late Upper Palaeolithic flints recently discovered near Towler Hill, on a series of river terraces above the river Tees. The latter included blade forms and points, known as 'Creswellian points', that are diagnostic of this period. In addition, a range of very heavily patinated flaked flints have been found re-chipped into Mesolithic tools, associated with a site that has been dated to *c.*7800 BC on the Northumberland coast at Howick. It is clear that these pieces originate from a much earlier period, probably the Upper Palaeolithic. Some of them are beach-rolled, which implies they have come from land under what is now the North Sea and were washed on to the Howick shoreline. Here they were collected and re-chipped, a phenomenon observed in many Mesolithic assemblages from the north-east coast, and indirect evidence for earlier, probably late Upper Palaeolithic, activity along the coastline and on the land that now lies immediately off-shore.

It seems that people may have made the occasional foray into the glacial and tundra wastes of this region towards the end of the last Ice Age, although on account of the remarkably few finds of this date it appears that such visits were short-lived, sporadic and small-scale. However, the

17 A probable Late Upper Palaeolithic blade from near Prudhoe

coast of Norway was colonised in the late Upper Palaeolithic so there is no reason why the same should not have taken place in northern Britain. The lack of evidence here is no doubt intimately linked to processes of environmental and sea-level change that have led to widespread erosion of the east coast shoreline and the submergence of sites below the sea.

Mesolithic

Mesolithic means 'Middle Stone Age' and is the name given to the period from the end of the last Ice Age to the beginning of farming, roughly 10,000-4000 BC in the British Isles. It is divided into early and late Mesolithic, respectively covering the colder post-glacial period before about 8200 BC and the warm temperate period after that date. The inhabitants of this land were hunters, gatherers and fishers who adapted to and exploited the landscape without recourse to farming. The post-glacial hunters of the early Mesolithic were reliant on large animals, such as elk, red deer, wild cattle and horse, as well as some smaller mammals, such as mountain hare and pine marten. This gave rise to a distinctive stone tool kit and way of life that involved following herds as they moved around the landscape. There are no remains yet radiocarbon-dated to this period in Northumberland, although it is likely that some of the stone tools that have been found could date to this time.

As the climate warmed up a dramatic change took place over Northumberland; new plant species colonised the area eventually giving rise to massive broad-leaf forests, dominated by oak and elm, that supported a much greater diversity of flora and fauna. This meant that the land could not only sustain a larger human population but it also provided a much wider variety of foodstuffs, such as freshwater and saltwater fish, a wider range of mammals, including fox and boar, as well as many more bird species and plant foods. At the same time, animals such as elk and horse that are not suited to a wooded environment eventually became extinct in this area. It is during this period of the rich primeval woodlands that the story of Northumberland's Mesolithic begins to unfold.

Tools and Technology

Typically there are very few remains surviving from this period, particularly in the way of structures, although we assume the Stone Age people of the Mesolithic utilised a wide range of naturally occurring materials in order to make tools, equipment, clothing, bedding and structures. These would have included bark, timber, leaves, grass, roots, plant stems, turf, stone, hide, bone, horn, antler, shell, feathers and many more. The environment was both a store cupboard and workshop that people lived in, not an alien surrounding that people lived separately from, as we largely do today. Very few of these perishable materials survive in the British climate and soils, although occasionally such finds are recovered from favourable settings such as waterlogged environments. For example, a fishing harpoon made from antler was found washed up on the coast at Whitburn and can be seen in the Museum of Antiquities at Newcastle.

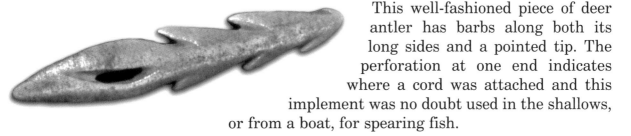

This well-fashioned piece of deer antler has barbs along both its long sides and a pointed tip. The perforation at one end indicates where a cord was attached and this implement was no doubt used in the shallows, or from a boat, for spearing fish.

18 An antler harpoon point from Whitburn

The best preserved tools, though, are the stone implements which have been found in their thousands across most parts of Northumberland. Since stone tools were the main technology of the Mesolithic and are virtually indestructible, archaeologists have become reliant on the examination of them to build up an understanding of this period. Studies of Mesolithic collections have shown that people in Northumberland relied to a great extent on locally available stone to make their tools. As a result Mesolithic stone tools are made from a

19 Beach flint from Northumberland

wide range of rock types including flint, chert, agate and quartz. Flint can be found most easily along the coast where it is washed on to the beach from offshore deposits. In addition, the boulder clays that mantle the north-east coastal plain also contain secondary flint deposits and nodules can be collected from erosion scars on valley sides, or from the beach where the till erodes into the sea. The coastal and glacial flint can be quite distinctive and includes grey-orange, bright orange, and speckled red-brown varieties, as well as flints of various shades of grey.

Flint can also be obtained from gravel deposits in the major river basins including, in particular, the Tyne and Till valleys. Chert is usually found in association with limestone deposits and in north Northumberland cherts of various types, including a distinctive blue-grey variety, have been used to make Mesolithic tools. The brightly coloured banded agates can also be found in the gravel deposits, whereas quartz can be found all over Northumberland in tills, gravels and other secondary geological deposits.

During the Mesolithic the hunter-gatherers adopted a flaking technology that revolved around the produc-tion of blades. Blades are long, thin flakes, often with parallel sides. This is an economical way of flaking stone as it ensures that the

20 Microliths made from agate, chert and quartz from the Milfield basin

number of tools that can be made from a flint core is maximised. The characteristic stone tool associated with blade production in this period is the 'microlith' (meaning small stone).

Microliths are very small blades that have been delicately chipped along their edges to produce barbs of particular shapes. Although used in a wide range of tools they are most often associated with hunting weapons. A number of microliths would be hafted on to a weapon, such as a wooden spear or arrow shaft, forming sharp armatures for cutting through flesh. The microliths were fixed in position using resin from trees such as Scots Pine, or tied with leather cord. Occasionally rare examples of hafted microliths survive in waterlogged conditions and have confirmed their use as hunting weapons.

21 Different types of late Mesolithic microliths made from flint

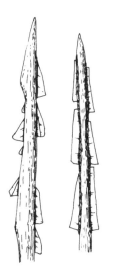

22 Microliths are used in composite tools such as these two examples from the continent

As microliths formed parts of composite tools, if one of the barbs broke, or became dislodged, another could easily be attached. This made microliths very efficient as it meant that hunting gear could be quickly and easily repaired without having to make an entire new tool. Microliths from the early Mesolithic tend to be broader, larger and irregular in shape, whereas those from the later Mesolithic tend to be smaller, narrower and more geometric. This change in the tool kit is thought to be related to changes in the type of animals being taken, as well as in the hunting strategies employed.

It is amazing just how many different tools can be made from stone, and how it can be worked and utilised in different ways. During the Mesolithic flint axes were used for felling trees while engraving tools, referred to as 'burins', were used for working bone and antler. Small retouched stub-ended flakes were used to scrape the skins of dead animals as part of the hide preparation process. These tools are referred to as 'scrapers' and are frequently found at settlement sites.

Other types of flints, such as 'primary flakes', are associated with the initial chipping and preparation stages of the raw material, and these are typically found close to flint collection sites. A fieldwalking project undertaken by Alan Williams around Chevington, near the Northumberland coast, produced the highest proportion of flints per

23 Top row: late Mesolithic microliths. Bottom row: early Mesolithic microliths

hectare than anywhere else in the north-east and many were associated with this preliminary stage of stone tool working. They included many rough flakes with the coarse outer crust ('cortex') of the flint surviving on one side, as well as nodules that had been tested, and some prepared cores. The high density of primary chippings suggests that this area was visited for the collection and initial preparation of flint during Mesolithic times. The prepared pieces would then be taken back to settlement sites where the flint cores would be flaked to produce blanks that could be made into the tools required for day-to-day activities.

24 A flint scraper being used to clean the fat from a deer skin

25 A selection of flint scrapers

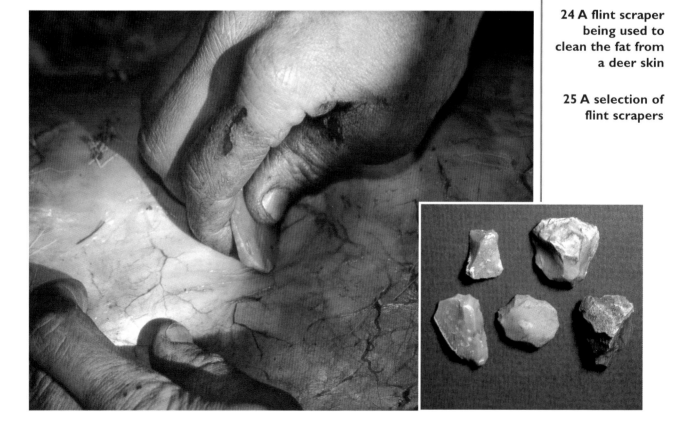

26 View from the Corby's Crag rock shelter site

Settlement

Hunter-gatherers are widely regarded as leading mobile lives, wandering around the landscape in order to take advantage of seasonal abundance in different places. As a result, hunter-gatherers are thought to have lived a footloose existence using lightly built, mobile shelters, though no evidence of these has yet been found in Northumberland. Based on analogies with modern hunter-gatherer groups it is generally thought that Mesolithic people lived in small groups who resided at 'base camps'. On occasions some members would form a 'task group' to hunt and forage further afield and bring supplies back to the base camp. These smaller groups would stay in short-stay shelters referred to as 'logistical camps'. In Northumberland evidence for short-stay logistical camps has been discovered along the foot of a number of sandstone crags, such as Corby's Crag and Dove Crag.

Excavations by Colin Burgess at Goatscrag recovered evidence for Mesolithic occupation that included not just flint tools associated with hunting gear, but also some gullies, slots and post sockets that appear to have been used to construct a shelter against the rock overhang. What is more, there are the unmistakable images of four deer-like animals engraved into the sandstone face within the rock shelter.

27 Carvings inside a Mesolithic rock shelter at Goatscrag thought to depict deer

These engravings may or may not date to the Mesolithic, but their presence within the rock shelter, and the style of the images, make it highly unlikely that this is mere coincidence. Maybe the images were made by hunters who sought assistance through some kind of sympathetic magic, or maybe they were the idle art of a hunting group anticipating the chase. Whatever the meaning behind this representational rock art, if it is Mesolithic, not only would it be some of the oldest art in Britain but it would also tell us something about the people who used the rock shelters. If the interpretation of the images is correct then it supports the archaeological evidence that this was a logistical camp used by hunters. Furthermore, the site occupies high ground overlooking a narrow valley leading into the fertile lands of the Milfield plain. This valley would have formed a natural routeway for migrating herds seeking lush vegetation and fresh water. Therefore, the rock outcrop occupies a strategic location ideally suited for observing and intercepting animals on the hoof. The red deer was one of the largest animals hunted for meat throughout the Mesolithic and bringing down one of these majestic creatures must have been a significant achievement and important event. It can be fairly assumed, then, that the role of the deer-hunter had great potency in Mesolithic society and helped to define the status of the individual. Mesolithic face-masks made from red deer skulls, found at Star Carr in North Yorkshire, add to this sense of importance, and perhaps indicate a ritual connection between these Stone Age hunters and the king of the forest.

28 Red Deer stag - one of the largest animals hunted for meat in the Mesolithic

Other rock shelter sites in Northumberland that have produced evidence for short-lived Mesolithic occupations include the site excavated by Stan Beckensall at Corby's Crag outside Alnwick and the discovery of flints at the foot of Bowden Doors and Colourheugh Crags by climbers. Other upland sites, thought to be of a logistical nature, have been discovered elsewhere in the county. For example, Chris Tolan-Smith has excavated a site on Birkside Fell in the North Pennines where hundreds of Mesolithic flint tools have been found eroding from the exposed peat.

The evidence for base camps in Northumberland, as with the rest of the country, has been very much lacking until the recent discovery of a site at Howick on the Northumberland coast. This site was found by field-workers John Davies and Jim Hutchinson who noticed flint tools eroding out of the cliff edge. The finds were brought to the attention of one of the authors (CW) and the site was excavated over two seasons during 2000 and 2002. Incredibly, the site had survived virtually intact until the cliff erosion took place. The excavations revealed evidence for a circular sunken-floored hut with post sockets and post pads for timbers that had supported a conical roof. The hut measured 6m in diameter and would have been sufficient for a family to live in. These are the first definite structural remains for a Mesolithic base camp so far found in Northumberland. The initial construction of the site has been radiocarbon-dated to around 7800 BC so there is no doubt about its Mesolithic date.

The position of this site close to the Mesolithic shoreline is interesting as the climate here would have been more moderate than further inland. It is generally warmer in winter and colder in summer, and so does not experience the extremes that occur in areas such as the Cheviot uplands. Furthermore, the coast is an extremely rich environment with access to fish, shellfish, seaweed, fowl, nesting birds and seals, as well as being in reach of land-based fauna, such as deer, wild pig and wild cattle, and many plant foods, such as nuts, berries, fruits and a range of green leafy plants. The coast would, therefore, make an ideal place to stay over the long winter months when food is harder to come by. The site at Howick revealed evidence for the gathering of hazelnuts on a massive scale as well as the taking of wild pig, fox, birds and grey seal. The bones of either a wolf or dog were also found. A domesticated dog was found at the Star Carr site too, which shows that people had already tamed dogs and had no doubt adopted them as hunting companions. Taking this evidence into account, we can be fairly confident that the Howick site served as a base camp, at least over the winter months, as hazelnuts ripen in the autumn. Further support for the location of base camps near the coast has recently been discovered to the north of Berwick at Dunbar, where a very similar Mesolithic hut with post sockets has just been excavated by John Gooder. Although we must be careful not to generalise for Northumberland as a whole, it appears that, for the area of coastal mid-Northumberland, Mesolithic people were living for part, if not all, of the year around the coast, with

29 The excavations at Howick took place on a headland overlooking the rocky coastline

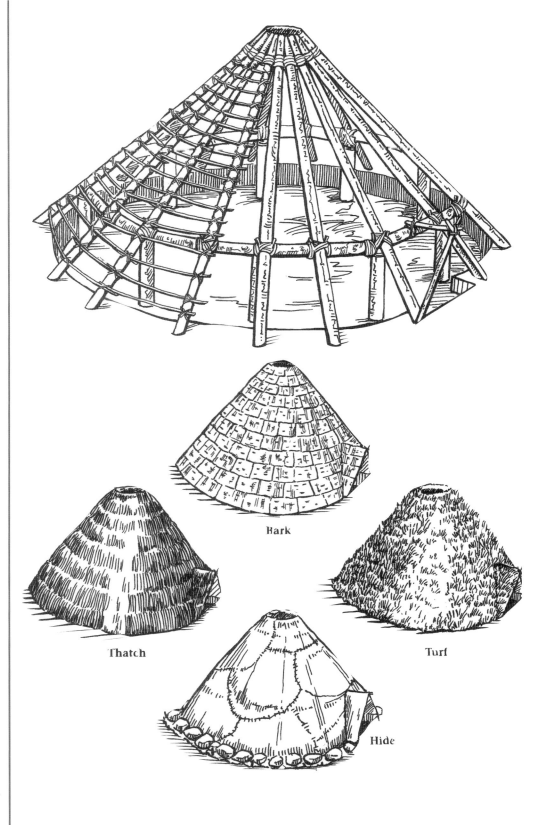

Bark

Thatch

Turf

Hide

30 Whilst the timber fame is based on archaeological evidence the hut may have been covered in a variety of materials

hunting groups foraging inland using shelters such as Corby's Crag to take game – possibly as a summer activity.

Recent fieldwork in the Milfield basin, however, has shown that some Mesolithic groups also occupied fertile river valleys inland, where they may have lived year-round. In the case of the Milfield area, this inland river basin forms an interface between different geological environments which allows access to different resources during the changing seasons of the year. This could include game-hunting in the uplands during summer, collection of nuts and berries in the lower-lying forested areas during autumn, and the taking of beasts such as wild boar in the more sheltered areas during winter. Furthermore, the rivers that converge in this flood basin would have provided rich stocks of fish as well as wildfowl, nesting birds and plant foods. Being situated in the rain shadow of the Cheviot massif the basin, like the coast, enjoys a moderate climate.

...continued on page 33

31 The rich agricultural land of the Milfield plain is home to a wealth of Mesolithic archaeology

The Howick Hut

One of the most important Mesolithic sites excavated in recent years is that at Howick. Preserved at the site were the remains of a circular hut that had three successive structural phases, being rebuilt on exactly the same footprint each time. Radiocarbon dates from throughout the stratigraphic sequence have shown that the site was occupied for around 150 years and is likely to have been home to several generations of the same family group.

32 The remains of the Mesolithic hut after complete excavation

The excavation of the site was incredibly painstaking as many of the features survived as stains in the sand. This meant the structural remains were often recognised only as subtle changes in texture, colour and compaction. Every archaeological layer had to be planned, recorded and photographed before excavating further. The entire contents of every archaeological feature were passed through a flotation tank with built-in sieve in order to recover organic remains, such as charred material, bone and shell, and inorganic finds, such as small pieces of flint and ochre.

33 Over a million charred hazelnut shells were recovered by careful sieving of the hut sediments

One of the most important discoveries at Howick was the survival of a series of hearth pits in the centre of the hut. These hearths had preserved the charred remains of meals from almost 10,000 years ago. Most of them contained charred hazelnut shells, while in others small burnt bone fragments survived. These included the paw bones of fox and either dog or wolf, as well as evidence for wild pig, birds and seal. This range of mammals includes very different types of creature, implying some were caught for their pelts while others were taken for their meat, skins or even feathers, in the case of the birds. Being close to a cliff edge it can be fairly assumed that the inhabitants of the site also caught fish, though fish bones are notoriously poor survivors on archaeological sites. The occasional shell was found in the archaeological sediments hinting at the exploitation of shellfish living on the nearby rocky shore.

Over 13,000 struck flints were found in the hut. These included a wide range of tools such as microliths, scrapers, burins, piercers and sharpened flakes and blades, which are just the kinds of processing tools that would be expected at a base camp. Another common find on the site was fragments of red ochre, which is a form of haematite. This is used by some indigenous tribes as a sun block and to keep insects

34 Section through charred deposits in a cooking pit

off the skin, while others use it in medicine, as it has antiseptic qualities and helps to staunch bleeding; others still use it as a pigment for making up paint. Body painting is well known amongst hunter-gatherer groups who can create different colours by heat-treating ochre.

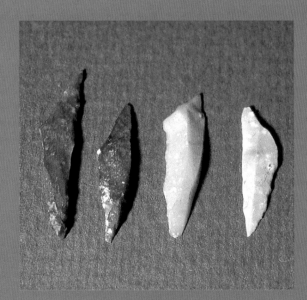

35 Microliths from Howick probably used as barbs in hunting weapons

Using the archaeological evidence, the Howick hut was 'reconstructed' in an attempt to visualise what it may have looked like when complete. The first stage was to dig out the sunken floor and erect the timber uprights. The roof timbers were then tied on using plant fibre cord and this provided a frame on to which a thatch of wild grass was attached. The choice of roof covering is conjectural, with other candidates being reed thatch, bark or turf. A hide cover is thought unlikely as the hut would not have been as solidly constructed if it only had to support a skin roof. Once built, the hut was found to be spacious, warm and a suitable size for a group of 6 to 8 people. The pitch of the roof is certainly too shallow, but if an angle of around 60° was used, as suggested at the site, this would make the apex of the reconstruction around 5m above the ground surface.

36 - 37
The reconstruction of the Howick hut

38 Flintknapper John Lord making stone tools inside the reconstructed hut

...Continued from page 28

During much of the Mesolithic, south-eastern Britain remained connected to the Continent by a land bridge extending from Lincolnshire and East Anglia over to the Low Countries. The North Sea was a huge basin open only to the north. Large islands existed within this basin, with one in the area of the Dogger Bank perhaps as large as modern-day Denmark. Archaeological remains in the form of harpoon points and flints have been retrieved from these submerged banks, brought up by fishnets, dredging and oil cores. The Northumberland coast would have looked out to a distant archipelago with a coastline running south then east, all the way to the Baltic. Transport across the sea, by island-hopping or coast-hugging in skin boats, was probably easier and more efficient than movement through the thick forests that covered much of Britain at this time.

Subsistence

The diet of Britain's Stone Age hunter-gatherers was probably more rich and varied than we would expect. By the later Mesolithic the land supported diverse habitats within its vast woodlands, but there were also areas of grassland, scrub, peat and some moorland. Archaeologists have traditionally seen Mesolithic groups as being largely dependent on hunting, particularly deer, with some gathered resources such as nuts and berries to pad out the diet. But this model is an inaccurate generalisation that fails to account for the wide range of options available to groups living in different environmental settings, as well as the changing availability of a wide range of foods throughout the year.

In Northumberland there is emerging evidence to suggest that marine resources were an important source of food for Mesolithic groups. At Low Hauxley, near Amble, a midden site was discovered eroding out of the cliff during high tides. Investigations at the site revealed a substantial deposit of shell remains associated with charcoal and flint. This heap of refuse provides evidence for the collection of shellfish that could have been consumed for food and/or used as bait. The midden probably has fish bones too, but it has not yet been fully investigated. As the coast has been eroded, the midden sites that probably dotted the Mesolithic shoreline have, by and large, been destroyed. However, direct evidence for sea fishing is provided by the bone harpoon point from Whitburn.

Some indirect evidence for marine exploitation is suggested by the presence of a particular type of stone tool associated with coastal sites. Coarse 'bevelled pebbles' have been found at a number of Northumbrian sites, including Howick and Ness End quarry on Holy

Island. At one time these tools were thought to be hammers or scoops for removing limpets from rocks, but now most archaeologists regard them as being too heavy and impractical for this task. Instead, there is a growing opinion that they were associated with the scraping of seal skins, as flint tools are probably too sharp for the soft coat. A study of the Welsh evidence identified a possible correlation between the distribution of bevelled tools and the location of seal breeding grounds and the Howick site, with its 33 bevelled tools, seal bones from a hearth and the seal breeding grounds at the base of the cliffs, ties in well with this view.

Wild cattle bones have been found in the submerged Mesolithic forest on the beach at Seaton Carew, Hartlepool, while the evidence from Howick reveals the exploitation of wild pig, fox and birds. Although no evidence of deer has yet been recovered, by analogy with other sites, such as Star Carr, we can be sure that deer formed an important staple in the Mesolithic diet of the region. Some of the pollen diagrams relating to the uplands of Northumberland and surrounding areas have revealed evidence for episodes of localised woodland clearance during the Mesolithic. This is thought to be a result of human activity, as clearing woodland allows the ground flora to regenerate and the new shoots attract forest browsers, particularly deer and wild cattle. By managing the woodland in this way hunters could attract large game to certain areas, which would allow hunting to be geared around predictable locations. Such strategies would also enable Mesolithic groups to maintain their hunting territories by attracting game away from areas of woodland that were being over-grazed. This would ensure the renewal of vegetation and the long-term viability of the environment and their hunter-gatherer way of life.

© Peter Evans

Gathered resources include the hazelnut, ever present on Mesolithic sites, which appears to have been purposely harvested at Howick. However, other foods would include berries and fruits, as well as roots and edible green leafy plants. Rock carvings in Scandinavia include images of people obtaining honey, and this must have formed one of the most highly prized foods in the Mesolithic as there were few sweet foods available at this time.

...continued on page 37

39 Chilllingham Wild Cattle are the nearest surviving relatives to the ancient beasts that once roamed the landscape

Case Study: Fieldwalking

Fieldwalking is a key archaeological technique employed to locate sites and map patterns of human activity over large areas of landscape. It involves walking in a systematic fashion over ploughed fields and recording any artefacts that may be found. This technique allows artefact scatters to be located, which are then recorded on field plans.

40 Fieldwalking involves inspecting the surface for artefacts

As stone tools survive so well, fieldwalking is one of the most common ways by which flints are collected and Stone Age sites identified. In Northumberland there have been some important large-scale fieldwalking projects in the Milfield basin, the Tyne valley and the Shaftoe-Bolam area, as well as smaller-scale surveys, particularly along the coast.

41 A freshly ploughed and weathered surface provides the ideal conditions for discovering finds

Fieldwalking involves walking in straight lines across a field with walkers set at regular distances, usually 5m or 10m apart. Finds are marked with a bamboo cane and the location recorded with a surveying instrument (usually a total station). The finds are then bagged and labelled with a number corresponding to the survey point, before being washed and dried ready for examination.

42 Once artefacts have been discovered their position is carefully recorded

The different finds are then examined and their details recorded. This allows field plots to be made showing the distribution of different types of finds belonging to different periods. These distribution maps can be used to identify different types of sites and activities that may have taken place. This information can in turn be used to devise a programme of more detailed examination, which could include excavation. One of the problems with fieldwalking, though, is that artefact distributions can be affected by processes which bias the data. For example, artefact densities observed at the base of a slope may have gathered there as a result of movement downslope during heavy rain. Alternatively, apparent blanks in some fields may be the result of masking of remains by alluvium. It is therefore essential that such factors are taken into account when interpreting fieldwalking results.

Fieldwalking finds are a resource in themselves and can provide a generalised picture of human activity over a wide landscape. This is ideally suited for reconstructing hunter-gatherer behaviour as it allows their activities to be mapped at a landscape scale, which corresponds well with the way these people lived their lives and used their environment.

43 Stone tools found by fieldwalking at Howick

...Continued from page 34

Social Organisation, Life and Death

As the archaeological remains for this period are so scant we are limited in what can be reliably stated about Mesolithic social organisation. One thing is clear though: if the Howick hut is anything to go by, it appears that Mesolithic groups organised themselves in small family units of around half a dozen people or so, who lived together for much of the year. The presence of short-stay logistical camps, however, indicates that small groups of perhaps two or three individuals split off from such family groups at certain times, in search of prey and other resources. If anthropological studies of native American Indians are anything to go by then it is likely that these task groups were made up mostly, or wholly, of males. Families would not have lived in isolation all year round, however, and anthropological studies show that groups are likely to have come together at certain times as part of a larger band in order to celebrate festivals, carry out rituals, exchange goods, acquire marriage partners, cement social bonds, meet friends and extended family and share news.

We know very little about how these hunter-gatherers disposed of their dead as there have been few finds of Mesolithic burials anywhere in Britain. This absence of bodies implies that Mesolithic people either cremated their dead or perhaps left them out to be consumed by wild animals or carrion. Based on studies of modern hunter-gatherer tribes around the world, archaeologists usually assume that their world-view was formed around a perception of people being part of the natural world and not separate from it in the way that we look at things today. Such a view, it could be argued, is consistent with the exposure of corpses to carrion and other predators, as this practice allows the corpse to return to nature by sustaining other birds and animals. If, however, the hunter-gatherers had systematically buried their dead, so as to preserve the corpse in perpetuity as an intact human entity, then this would perhaps signal a separation between people on the one hand and the rest of the natural world on the other, as in the modern Judaeo-Christian-Muslim world-view. The absence of burials in the Northumberland Mesolithic may then tell us something about how these hunter-gatherers related to the world.

Further Reading

General
Barton, R. N. E. 1997. *Stone Age Britain.* London: B.T. Batsford and English Heritage.
Coles, B. 1998. Doggerland: A speculative survey. *Proceedings of the Prehistoric Society* 64: 45-81.

Morrison, A. 1980. *Early Man in Britain and Ireland*. London: Croom Helm Ltd.

Simmons, I. G. 1996. *The Environmental Impact of Later Mesolithic Cultures*. Edinburgh: Edinburgh University Press.

Smith, C. 1992. *Late Stone Age Hunters of the British Isles*. London: Routledge.

Waddington, C. 2004. *The Joy of Flint*. Newcastle: Society of Antiquaries of Newcastle-upon-Tyne.

Wymer, J. 1991. *Mesolithic Britain*. Princes Risborough: Shire.

Northumberland

Beckensall, S. 1976. The excavation of a rock shelter at Corby's Crags, Edlingham. *Archaeologia Aeliana* 5th ser. 4: 11-16.

Buckley, F. 1922. Early Tardenois remains at Bamburgh. *Proceedings of the Society of Antiquaries of Newcastle upon Tyne* 3rd ser. 10: 319-23.

Buckley, F. 1925. The microlithic industries of Northumberland. *Archaeologia Aeliana* 4th ser. 1: 42-7.

Burgess, C. B. 1972. Goatscrag, A Bronze Age rock shelter cemetery in North Northumberland. *Archaeologia Aeliana* 4th ser. 50: 15-69.

Mellars, P. 1970. An antler harpoon-head of 'Obanian' affinities from Whitburn, County Durham. *Archaeologia Aeliana* 4th ser. 48: 337-46.

Mulholland, H. 1970. The microlithic industries of the Tweed valley. *Transactions of the Dumfriesshire and Galloway Natural History and Antiquarian Society* 3rd ser. 47: 81-110.

O'Sullivan, D. and R. Young 1995. *Lindisfarne. Holy Island*. London: B.T. Batsford.

Tolan-Smith, C. 1996. The Mesolithic/Neolithic Transition in the Lower Tyne Valley: a Landscape Approach. *Northern Archaeology* (Special Edition) 13-14: 7-15.

Tolan-Smith, C. 1997. The Stone Age Landscape: the Contribution of Fieldwalking. In Tolan-Smith (ed.) *Landscape Archaeology in Tynedale*. Newcastle upon Tyne: University of Newcastle upon Tyne: 79-89.

Trechmann, C. T. 1936. Mesolithic Flints from the Submerged Forest at West Hartlepool. *Proceedings of the Prehistoric Society* 2: 161-8.

Waddington, C. 1999. *A Landscape Archaeological Study of the Mesolithic-Neolithic in the Milfield Basin, Northumberland*. Oxford: British Archaeological Reports, British Series 291.

Waddington, C. 2000. Recent research on the Mesolithic in the Milfield Basin, Northumberland. In R. Young (ed.) *Mesolithic Lifeways: Current Research in Britain and Ireland*. Leicester: Leicester Archaeology Monograph 5: 165-77.

Waddington, C., G. Bailey, *et al.* 2001. A Mesolithic settlement site at Howick, Northumberland: a preliminary report. *Archaeologia Aeliana* 5th Ser. 32: 1-12.

Weyman, J. 1975. Mesolithic occupation at Gallowhill Farm, Corbridge. *Archaeologia Aeliana* 5th Ser. 3: 219-20.

Weyman, J. 1980. A flint chipping site at Low Shilford, Riding Mill, Northumberland. *Archaeologia Aeliana* 5th Ser. 8: 159-61.

Weyman, J. 1984. The Mesolithic in North-East England. In R. Miket and C. Burgess (eds.) *Between And Beyond The Walls: Essays in Honour of George Jobey*. Edinburgh: John Donald: 38-51.

Young, R. 1984. Potential Sources of Flint and Chert in the North-East of England. *Lithics* 5: 3-9.

Young, R. 2000. Aspects of the 'coastal Mesolithic' of the north east of England. In R. Young (ed.) *Mesolithic Lifeways. Current Research from Britain and Ireland*. Leicester: University of Leicester Archaeology Monographs No. 7: 179-190.

Young, R., D. Coggins and T. Laurie 1989. The late Upper Palaeolithic and Mesolithic of the North Pennine Dales in the light of recent research. In C. Bonsall (ed.) *The Mesolithic in Europe: Proceedings of the 3rd International Mesolithic Symposium, Edinburgh*, 164-174.

4 Early Neolithic

The early Neolithic is the period associated with the first farming groups and dates from *c*.4000-3200 BC. Many archaeologists now think that the changes that took place around 4000 BC did not simply include new methods of obtaining food, but also a new ideology that changed how people related to the natural world. One function of this ideological change was, no doubt, to legitimise the taming of animals and plants and sanction a new way of living in the world. Once people became tied to the land then concepts of ownership, competition for resources, wealth and control over the natural world would have emerged. This profound shift in the way people thought and lived would have required a persuasive ideological underpinning if it was to take hold and prevent people from returning to hunter-gatherer ways. Anthropological studies have shown that, in general, when groups take up farming they tend to get locked in and find it very difficult to revert to a hunter-gatherer mode of existence both for practical and social reasons. Such fundamental change no doubt raised tensions

"Herders and Agriculturalists"

between groups, and some archaeologists have drawn attention to the adoption of arrowheads and the numbers in which they occur at this time. Furthermore, many of these distinctive leaf-shaped arrowheads have been found associated with enclosure entrances, which appear to have been attacked, or lodged in human corpses left in the enclosure ditches. Far from being a time of peaceful co-existence, the insecurities of a society grappling with this new ordering of the world and inter-group competition appear to have sometimes spilled over into outright warfare.

One of the big questions facing archaeologists is whether the adoption of farming came about as a result of mass incursions of farming people from the Continent, or whether the indigenous hunter-gatherer groups adopted it themselves. These two views represent the extreme poles of the argument and many prehistorians think that the spread of the ideas

44 Leaf - shaped arrowheads are classic early Neolithic finds

associated with farming and taming the natural world was just as important as any physical movement of people. Domesticated animals must have been transported across the North Sea, however, which means physical contact with farming groups from the Continent must have taken place. Whether this involved wholesale migrations is another question. What is notable about the British Neolithic is that, as in the coastal margins of much of north-western Europe, it is different in many respects to the Neolithic of the rest of the Continent, and it also begins a thousand or so years later. Therefore, the hunter-gatherer populations of the British Isles and the north-western seaboard of Europe must have been aware of farming and its associated way of life for many hundreds of years, yet chose not to adopt it. This does not mean that these populations were in any way backward, but rather that they lived a successful and sustainable existence in what was probably a very abundant environment. There was no overriding need to adopt farming. Given that the Neolithic of Britain and the coastal areas of Western Europe have much in common in terms of burial practices, monuments and so forth at this time, it suggests that those hunter-gatherer people who occupied the Atlantic margin of Europe assimilated farming in their own distinctive way long after it had spread across much of the European landmass. If this is the case, then it would seem that the advent of the Neolithic lay partly in the arrival of newcomers, with their domestic crops and beasts, and partly in the decision to adopt this way of life at a certain time by indigenous hunter-gatherer groups. With the advent of oxygen isotope analysis, which allows the general place of a person's origin to be identified, it should be possible to answer this question more convincingly in the future.

Whatever happened around 4000 BC, it involved one of the most fundamental changes ever to take place in Britain. It included major technological developments, such as the first use of ceramics, as well as the intensification of food production, which allowed larger populations to be supported; and with more mouths to feed, more labour would have been needed to work the land. People, therefore, meant wealth, and wealth meant power, as surplus food could be exchanged for other materials such as flint and stone axes. This cycle of intensification appears to have led to competition for power, which is thought to lie behind the construction of the first monuments: long barrows and chambered tombs. These statements in stone and earth were the first permanent human constructions, signifying not only human control over the landscape but also territorial control by specific groups. It is in the maelstrom of these changing times, 6,000 years ago, that our modern concepts of the world were born.

Settlement

The structural evidence for early Neolithic settlements in the county consists of relatively flimsy structures that may not have been occupied all year round. Sites at Thirlings, in the Milfield basin, and near Bolam Lake produced trapezoidal and triangular arrangements of stone-packed postholes, together with a number of small stakeholes situated around them. The postholes were not the kind of massive features that could have supported a 'longhouse' of the proportions evidenced in areas of central Europe, but rather represent supports for less durable structures within short-lived settlements, perhaps occupied seasonally. The Bolam Lake site had a low hurdle fence associated with it that could not have served a defensive purpose but was an ideal size for keeping stock.

45 The excavated remains of a fence associated with a Neolithic settlement near Bolam Lake

The structure itself, like that at Thirlings, was not particularly robust and was probably put up quickly with the intention of being occupied for months rather than years. These sites are, therefore, suggestive of transitory camps rather than permanently occupied dwellings. The Bolam Lake site appears to have been a settlement for a herding group who may have occupied the camp during the summer months before shifting down to lower ground for over-wintering. At Thirlings there was evidence for grain processing and storage, so this group appears to have been more concerned with cultivated foods. As the structures here were evidently not permanent homes, it raises the question as to whether some groups involved with arable farming still retained a peripatetic existence and returned at certain times of the year to harvest their crops, rather than being permanently settled in one place. The continuation of some degree of residential mobility is also attested at other sites that have produced remains of Neolithic settlement activity.

Excavations at the Yeavering Henge site revealed evidence for earlier Neolithic settlement activity before the henge was built. The radiocarbon dates from these sites, and from Thirlings and Bolam Lake, all fall in the earlier half of the 4th millennium BC. At the Coupland site there were three pits that showed evidence for *in situ* burning, as the surrounding gravel had been scorched and fire-reddened. The pit fills were black in colour, being filled with charcoal, charred hazelnut shells, broken pottery and some burnt flints. These were thought to be cooking pits resulting from settlement activity at the site, though the settlements themselves had left no surviving trace in the substrata. These hearth pits are thought to be the remains of occasional stays by early Neolithic groups who lived in lightly-framed structures for short periods. Given the presence of hazelnuts on this site, together with other gathered foods at the Thirlings site, it is clear that some aspects of the hunter-gatherer lifestyle continued alongside this move to small-scale agriculture.

46 Excavations at the Coupland henge revealed evidence for an earlier settlement. This consisted of small hearth pits as shown in the inset

The view that many early Neolithic communities maintained a degree of mobility in their annual regime, particularly those inhabiting the uplands and their margins, is a view not shared by all archaeologists. Therefore, it is important to note that demonstrable evidence for more permanent Neolithic settlements has been discovered in other areas across Britain, such as at Skara Brae (Orkney) and Lismore Fields (Derbyshire), and that patterns of settlement during both the late Mesolithic and Neolithic may have varied widely across different regions. Such variability is no doubt linked to the availability of resources in any given landscape and the pervading social and cultural attitudes among the different tribes inhabiting the British Isles.

Continued on page 46...

Case Study: Bolam Lake

Local archaeologist John Davies has undertaken a large-scale fieldwalking programme in the Upper Wansbeck and Blyth valleys around the Bolam and Shaftoe areas. One field in particular caught his attention as not only did it contain an extraordinary concentration of flint artefacts but it also produced some early Neolithic pottery fragments. Armed with this information, John Davies and the author (CW) excavated an area of the pottery and flint scatter and in so doing discovered the remains of an early Neolithic settlement.

47 The Bolam Lake site during excavation with fence line in the foreground

After removal of the ploughsoil, the top of the subsoil was cleaned back to reveal a setting of stone-packed postholes that represented the remains of a settlement structure. More Neolithic pottery fragments were found associated with these structural remains, together with occasional pieces of flint. One of the posts had stood in an elongated pit with two massive stones placed around it for support. When excavated, the 'post-pipe' left by the timber could be seen between two stones, revealing the thickness of the post, in this case 0.12m in diameter.

48 Stone packing for a timber post

Immediately downwind of the structure was a series of pits containing what appears to be the domestic refuse of the Neolithic inhabitants. The pits contained many sherds of broken pottery, flints and charred hazelnut shells. This cluster of pits intercut, suggesting that the group may have returned to the site on several occasions. One pit, positioned slightly away from the others, had been cut into the sandstone bedrock and the degraded remains of an organic lining could be observed. It was therefore considered to have been a storage pit. However, a broken polished stone axe-head, made from Langdale tuff from the Lake District, was found at the base of the pit and may indicate the deliberate deposition of this object back into the ground. In other words, some of the artefact debris found in these pits may have been deposited in a ritualised way, rather than simply being discarded as rubbish.

49 A broken stone axe head found in the base of a rock-cut pit

On the opposite side of the structure, spreads of burnt material with associated postholes are thought to indicate where cooking had taken place and, beyond this, were the remains of a fenceline that appears to have run around the structure. When all this evidence is considered together it points towards a single family-sized settlement, probably belonging to a herding group. A few wheat and barley seeds were found in the rubbish pits, indicating this group had access to cereal crops, while the presence of charred hazelnuts indicates that they continued to gather food from nearby woodland. The presence of the fence is indicative of stock-keeping which, together with the other evidence, implies that this group enjoyed a wide variety of foods. The pottery fragments belong to robust coarseware pots that would have been used for cooking and storage.

The structure was 'reconstructed' as part of an archaeological experiment to find out just how robust it could have been. The work was carried out at the Brigantium Archaeological Centre in Redesdale. The timber frame made from birch was put up within a few hours and a turf roof laid during subsequent days. It was clear that the frame was too weak to have supported such a roof as it fell in shortly afterwards. It was concluded that the original hut must have been roofed with a lighter covering, such as hides. If it had been skin-covered the entire settlement could have been put up in less than a day and this is in keeping with the needs of a small mobile family group concerned with moving stock to the uplands for grazing. Without the experiment this important finding would not have come to light and the site could have been misinterpreted.

50 The reconstruction of the Neolithic hut at Brigantium

...Continued from page 42

Bounding of Space: the first enclosures

It was during the Neolithic that the first enclosures were constructed. These monuments served to bound space and put into physical form the concepts of 'inside' and 'outside', and the notion of excluding the 'natural' wild world from the enclosed area within. These early enclosures were not originally built in a defensive way, though some were used for defence in their later phases. Part of their significance may have been associated with symbolically demarcating a human-controlled place from the outside world around it. Evidence for early Neolithic enclosures has, until recently, been confined to southern England but new evidence has shown that such enclosures also existed in the north, though they often take a slightly different form to their southern counterparts. Excavations on the magnificent Iron Age hillfort at Harehaugh, Coquetdale, revealed evidence for an earlier enclosure pre-dating the hillfort. A radiocarbon date from the soil horizon on which this original enclosure had been built dated its construction to around 3000 BC suggesting that it might be Neolithic.

Other sites are also known, such as a ditched enclosure on the Law Top at South Shields, below the Roman fort, and to the south a Neolithic style enclosure is visible as a series of cropmarks on aerial photographs of Hasting Hill in County Durham.

51 Section through the Harehaugh ramparts showing the buried soil horizon (the dark layer above the horizontal ranging pole)

Subsistence and Diet

Early Neolithic groups are thought to have been concerned with herding, particularly cattle and pig, in addition to varying intensities of cereal production, hunting and gathering. Evidence from excavations on early Neolithic settlement sites in Northumberland has shown that these cereal varieties included emmer wheat, barley and oats. This evidence for early Neolithic agriculture has received further support from high-resolution pollen studies undertaken in Redesdale and North Tynedale, which demonstrate the first cultivation of cereals in these valleys around 4000 BC. Other studies have noted pollen evidence for early Neolithic agriculture in some areas of the Cheviot Hills to the north. Quernstones, used for grinding grain into flour, have also been found at one of the Milfield sites, showing that people probably ate bread as one of their staples. At the same time wild nuts and berries, such as hazelnuts, hawthorn and bramble, were being collected and used on the same site. Elsewhere a recently discovered hurdle panel, radiocarbon-dated to around 3700 BC, and thought to have been used as part of a fish weir, has been found in the inter-tidal peat beds off Seaton Carew, Hartlepool. The many finds of leaf-shaped arrowheads across the north-east are testament to the continued importance of hunting, and probably also inter-group warfare, as mentioned above. Therefore, some Mesolithic subsistence practices appear to have continued side by side with the new farming strategies adopted by early Neolithic groups.

Tools and Technology

The production of pottery is an innovation associated with the onset of the Neolithic. Clay becomes ceramic (pottery) at around 550 - 600°C and this can be achieved in an open fire. In Northumberland these first ceramics have been found at a number of sites and all show the same basic characteristics. They are thick-walled, well-made vessels that have slightly out-turned, or rolled-over, rims. They are round-based and have a bag-shaped, or 'globular', form with a distinctive shoulder below the neck. The bag-shaped profiles of these pots are thought by some archaeologists to have evolved by copying the form of leather bags

52 Typical early Neolithic Grimston Ware pottery fragments from the Coupland site

previously used for cooking and storage.
This type of pottery is usually referred to
as 'Grimston Ware', after a site on the
Yorkshire Wolds where some of the
earliest finds were made. It rarely has
any decoration, and coarse grits,
usually crushed sandstone or quartz,
were included in the fabric as an
opening agent to prevent cracking of the
pot during firing. Many of the pot
fragments show evidence of burnishing;
this consists of smoothing of the pot
surface to make it watertight and provide
a more attractive finish. Being round-
based, these pots could be placed directly on
to a fire where they would make ideal cooking
vessels, particularly as the round base spreads heat evenly - in
much the same way as a wok. Although these pots are usually referred
to as coarsewares, they are well-made and robust.

53 A rim fragment
of an Impressed
Ware pot from
Kyloe Crags. This
style of pottery is
later than the
Grimston Ware
series pots dating
to around 3,000BC

Given that many of the fragments are around 6000 years old they have
done well to survive in the British environment. Indeed, many of these
sherds are preserved in a better state than Iron Age and early Medieval
pottery that is less than half their age. Analysis of microscopic organisms (diatoms), which occur in the clays used for making pots, has
allowed Alex Gibson to show that some early Neolithic pottery in the
Milfield basin utilised clay from the nearby river Till, thus demon-
strating local production.

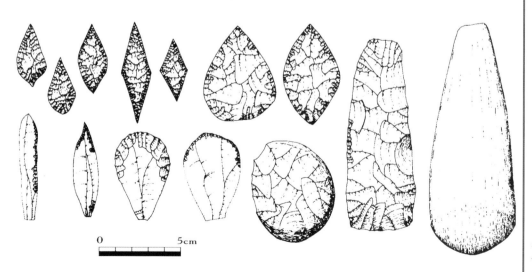

0   5cm

54 Typical flints
associated with
the early
Neolithic

The stone tool manufacturing traditions of the Mesolithic witnessed some radical innovations with the introduction of new tool forms and production techniques. At the same time, though, the blade-based technology was maintained, which reflects an important element of continuity with previous hunter-gatherer ways. Overall, the main features of the early Neolithic stone tool tradition are an increase in the variety of implements being produced, a change in sourcing to include large-scale flint mining and stone quarrying, and the use of new techniques such as grinding, polishing and invasive retouch (see flint-knapping case study below), together with more widespread use of pressure flaking. Typical forms associated with the early Neolithic include leaf-shaped arrowheads, laurel-leaf points, end-scrapers, serrated blades and flakes, and ground and polished stone axe-heads.

The finds of Fell sandstone, Whinstone and Cheviot andesite axe-heads demonstrate that various stone sources in north-east England were exploited during the Neolithic for axe production.

However, the provenancing of stone axe-heads in Northumberland has shown that the majority of axes were from Langdale in Cumbria, indicating the existence of long-distance exchange networks. Similarly, the use of nodular flint imported from the chalklands to the south becomes more widespread in the Neolithic. This flint is of a particularly high quality and had to be mined from large shafts cut into the chalk. It was often used to make especially fine pieces.

55 Axe heads made from local stone, in this case, andesite and sandstone respectively

It is perhaps significant that the main implements which changed between the late Mesolithic and early Neolithic periods were those generally thought to have been of most symbolic value, that is arrow-heads, axe-heads and cutting tools. The symbolic and ritual connotations of stone axe-heads are evidenced by intentional deposition in ceremonial and dedicatory contexts in and around early Neolithic enclosures, burial mounds and other ceremonial monuments, as well as in pits and ditch fills. For example, an important cache of stone axe-heads

Continued on page 54...

Case Study: Flintknapping

Flint is a type of silica (SiO_2), being composed of the elements silicon and oxygen. Although geologists continue to debate the matter, it is generally thought to form in deep-sea environments from silica-secreting organisms, and is thus a sedimentary rock. Being fine-grained, flint breaks in a regular and predictable way when it is struck. It fractures conchoidally which means that pieces of the nodule's shell detach in smooth curved flakes, the thickness and shape of which can be controlled. Removals frequently have a slightly crescentic profile.

Flintknapping is the art of flaking flint into stone tools. The process of fashioning a lump of flint, usually referred to as a 'nodule', into usable tools is termed the 'reduction sequence', or the 'chaîne opératoire'.

56-58 Flintknappers were adept at making sophisticated stone tools such as these edge-ground axe heads and sickles

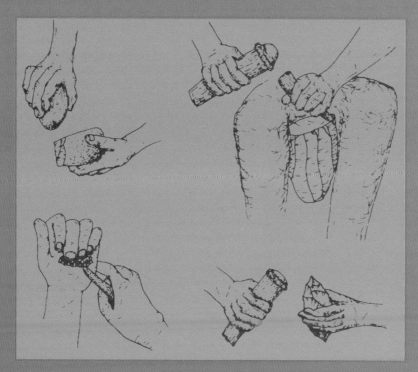

59 Different ways of flaking stone. From top left (clockwise): Hard hammer - direct percussion, Indirect percussion or 'antler punch' technique, Soft hammer - direct percussion and Pressure flaking

During the Neolithic this reduction sequence usually entailed the following steps:

1.   A flint nodule would have flakes removed to create a block from which further flakes could be removed in a more controlled manner. This block is referred to as a 'core'.

2.   The core is then carefully chipped to remove flakes that can be fashioned into tools. These flakes are termed 'blanks'.

3.   The blanks are very carefully chipped to create the desired shape and to sharpen, or blunt, edges. This careful chipping is called 'retouch'.

Flint can be knapped using a variety of techniques. Hard hammers, such as quartzite pebbles, are usually employed in the first stage of the reduction sequence to remove the large flakes. Soft hammers, usually an antler tine or wooden billet, are then used for lighter strikes that require greater control, such as the removal of blanks from a core. For the delicate retouch, however, a sharpened piece of antler or wood is placed against the blank surface and pressure applied until a piece is chipped off. This technique is known as 'pressure flaking' and allows much greater precision than the use of hammers. Another method by which precision work can be achieved is by 'indirect percussion', which involves using a punch placed against a blank surface and then striking the punch with a hammer. These different flaking methods can leave distinctive traces on stone tools. For example, the larger and more pronounced the bulb of percussion the harder the hammer used. Hard hammers may also leave traces of crushing at one end of the flake above the bulb of percussion.

As flint has to be chipped in a regular and predetermined way to produce the blanks needed to make stone tools, descriptive terms have been given to the different parts of a core and flake. The facet that is struck to detach flakes from a core is known as the 'striking platform'. The slightly raised bump on the inner face of the detached flake, caused by the hammer blow, is termed the 'bulb of percussion'. The struck end with the bulb of percussion is referred to as the 'proximal' end and the opposite end is the 'distal' end. The smooth inner side of the detached flake, that usually has evidence of ripples caused by the shock of the hammer blow, is known as the 'ventral' side, while the opposite side that has flaking scars, or the surviving outer crust of the flint ('cortex'), is the 'dorsal' side.

As flint fractures in a predictable way this means that, in theory, virtually any shape can be produced. The flintknapper's art reached its peak in the Neolithic and early Bronze Age when incredibly fine pieces were made. These range from small delicate arrowheads to large sickles and daggers. Flint is a wonderful material with a distinctive silky feel, shiny lustre and rich colours. Prehistoric people clearly appreciated its aesthetic qualities and it is quite common to find a particularly striking piece of flint specially selected to produce a particular tool.

During the Neolithic a new method of finishing flaked stone tools was introduced: the grinding and polishing of edges. By smoothing the edge of a tool this creates a more robust cutting edge as well as a different aesthetic appearance. Such 'edge-ground' tools typically include the blades of axe-heads and discoidal knives.

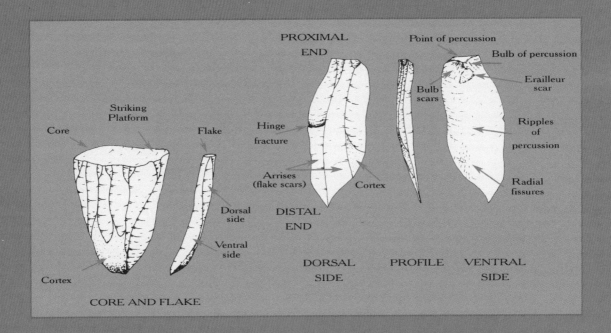

60 Diagram showing core and flake terminology

DATE Calendar years BC	ARCHAEO-LOGICAL PERIOD	CULTURAL TERMS	GEO-LOGICAL PERIOD	HOMINIDS	LITHIC TRADITIONS	EXAMPLES
1500 · 2500	Early Bronze Age				Wide variety of exotic tools. e.g. sickles and copies of metal objects such as daggers. Proliferation of poor quality flake tools for everyday use.	
2500 · 3200	Later Neolithic				Invasive retouch Flake tools and less reliance on blade technology Grinding and polishing	
3200 · 4000	Early Neolithic				Blade based industries Invasive retouch Grinding and polishing Platform cores Use of microliths abandoned Bifacial retouch common	
4000 · 8000	Later Mesolithic	Tardenoisian, Sauveterrian, and others.	↑		Narrow blade microliths Geometric microliths Abrupt retouch, usually unifacial only Platform cores	
8000 · 10000	Early Mesolithic	Maglemosian, Azilian, and others.	Flandrian/ Holocene		Broad blade microliths Burins Abrupt retouch Blade tools Platform cores	
10000 · 15000	Late Upper Palaeolithic	Creswellian, Hamburgian, Magdalenian, and others.	Loch Lomond Stadial		Blade technology Creswellian points Cheddar points Platform cores	
15000 · 40000	Upper Palaeolithic	Magdalenian, Solutrean, Gravettian, Aurignacian, Châtelperronian, and others.	↑	Modern Homo Sapiens ↑	Blade technology Long blade tools including abrupt and invasive retouch. Unifacial and bifacial blade tools Laurel leaf points Shouldered points Burins	
40000 · 200000	Middle Palaeolithic	Mousterian	Devensian	Early Homo Sapiens (Neanderthals)	Flat based (bout coupé) hand axes Development of Levallois tradition Flake tools	
		Levallois	Ipswichian 120-110K			
200000 · 500000	Lower Palaeolithic	Acheulian	Wolstonian	Homo erectus (hominid) **Earliest known Palaeolithic occupation of Britain** ←	Hand axes and range of biface tools Scrapers	
			Hoxnian 250-350K			
			Anglian			
		Clactonian	Cromerian 350-500K			
500000 · 2000000		Oldowan		Homo habilis (hominid)	Core tools Pebble tools	

61 Table summarising flint types through the ages

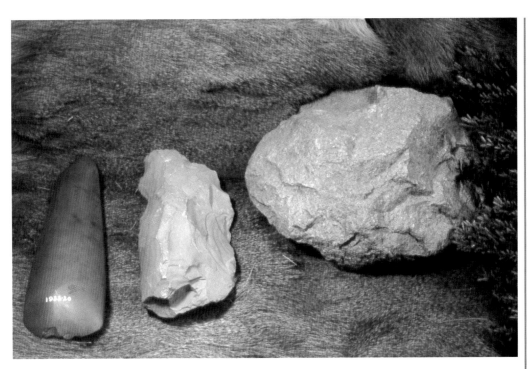

62 From right: a pounder, roughout and axe head - the latter two made from Langdale Tuff

...Continued from page 49

was found buried in what is understood to be a section of ditch in a resident's garden at Heddon-on-the-Wall, while others were found below an early Neolithic burial cairn on Broomridge to the west of Ford. The symbolic power of arrowheads, which can penetrate flesh and draw the life-blood from living things, has also been brought to the fore by ethnographic studies of modern-day aborigines. The new manufacturing methods, namely grinding and polishing and the use of invasive retouch, ensured that stone tools took on a more modified appearance. This suggests an intention to display them as overtly 'man-made' objects not of the 'natural' world. It has been suggested that these new methods and tool forms were as much about ways of producing explicitly cultural 'objects', physically and visually removed from their natural state, as they were innovations in stone tool technology.

Monuments in the Landscape

One of the defining features of the Neolithic is the construction of the first permanent structures that served to 'monumentalise' the landscape. In addition to the enclosures Neolithic groups also built formal burial structures, a phenomenon that marks an important departure from the preceding Mesolithic. In Northumberland these burial structures come in a wide variety of forms, from the long cairns and chambered cairns of Redesdale and North Tynedale, to the large round stone cairns, such as that on Broomridge near Ford, to small

63 The denuded remains of the Bellshiel long cairn

low cairns, such as that excavated on Chatton Sandyford Moor by George Jobey. Timber mortuary enclosures (ditched enclosures where rotting corpses were placed and sometimes buried) may also have been constructed but so far none of the suspected cropmark sites have been excavated.

Much debate surrounds why these structures were built, the functions they served, the rituals involved, and their ideological implications, but they are generally considered to have had a role connected with ancestor cults. Perhaps symbolising ancestral rites to certain areas of land, these monuments have recently been viewed as serving to 'presence' ancestors in the landscape. However, none of the large Northumbrian burial structures have been excavated in modern times and as a result little is known about the activities that took place there. It is somewhat unusual to have such a diversity of burial mound types within one area and this could suggest there were different regional groupings inhabiting different parts of Northumberland, or perhaps it relates to the availability of different building materials. Monument architecture plays an important role in framing human movement and focusing people's attention, particularly at places of religious significance. Therefore, the diversity of architecture witnessed in Northumberland implies that different ritual practices took place at the different monument types. Explaining this diversity remains a key question for understanding the early Neolithic in Northumberland.

Social Organisation

With the construction of formal monuments as permanent places in the landscape the early Neolithic inhabitants of Northumberland were laying down their claims to the land. Territories were marked out and rights of access to certain places, such as the enclosure sites and burial monuments, would have been controlled. The construction of these early monuments would have required the organisation of bigger groups than just family units and this implies that the actions of large numbers of people had to be co-ordinated. Such co-ordination necessitates leaders, and there can be little doubt that the Neolithic witnessed the emergence of social elites. At first these groupings may have been

Continued on page 59...

Case Study: Symbols on Stone

Another way of monumentalising the landscape, albeit in a less overt way than monument construction, was by engraving natural rock surfaces with symbolic art.

These designs are usually referred to as 'cup-and-ring marks' on account of the common use of hemispherical cup-shaped depressions surrounded by concentric rings. This type of artwork is abstract, having no figurative images associated with the many and varied compositions. Quite what these inscrutable symbols meant remains a mystery, although at a general level they are widely accepted as being associated with the belief systems of Neolithic groups.

64 Many cup and ring marked rocks, such as this on Dod Law, command wide views over the surrounding landscape

Although some contentions remain, many rock art scholars now accept that cup-and-ring marks, and cup marks certainly, were first deployed during the early Neolithic. In the past archaeologists were convinced that they were Bronze Age in origin, given their frequent associations with Bronze Age cairns. However, it is now realised that these rock sculptures were in use over a very long period extending from the 4th to the 2nd millennia BC. It is increasingly thought that the meanings associated with these motifs would have changed over time as they become deployed in different contexts during different periods. With art, and abstract symbols in particular, it is the context in which they are encountered that is the key to creating meaning. An example is the changing meaning of a cross, depending on the specific place that it is encountered (churches, national flags, first-aid kits, *etc.*). Cup-and-ring marks were first inscribed on naturally outcropping rock surfaces, usually on exposed slabs of bedrock on high ground in Northumberland. By the late Neolithic they became incorporated into ceremonial monuments, such as the cup-marked rock placed in a pit at the entrance of the Milfield South henge and the cup marks on the Duddo stone circle.

By the early Bronze Age, cup-and-ring-marked rocks are found exclusively associated with burial cairns. A number of cist slabs had designs carved on their surfaces, though these were always positioned to face inwards towards the corpse. In other cases, such as at Fowberry, a cairn (thought to have been for burial, though no bones survived) containing small cup-marked stones as part of the cairn material, was constructed over an earlier cup-and-ring-marked rock outcrop.

What is a symbol? A symbol is a form of sign whose meaning is implied rather than stated. It does not signify precisely in the way that the written word or spoken language can but may convey a suite of meanings with different emphasis at different

© Museum of Antiquities

65 Some carved panels, such as this from Stamfordham, were later re-used as grave covers in the early Bronze Age

times. In this way symbols stimulate an intuitive and personalised understanding without necessarily defining, or constraining, a concept or belief. Furthermore, because of their ambiguity symbols have the ability to convey large amounts of complex information in a concise way, while at the same time transcending the barrier of language. It is perhaps this direct engagement with the minds of Neolithic people that makes these symbols so attractive to us today.

The wealth of rock art in Northumberland makes it one of the key areas for studying this phenomenon in Britain. It occurs from the Peak District in the south to Argyll in the north, and from Ireland in the west to Northumberland and the North Yorkshire Moors in the east. It can also be found on the margins of Atlantic Europe with a particular concentration known in Galicia, Spain. This distribution suggests shared ideas across a wide area from the Neolithic onwards and may even hint at early cultural affiliations. There is plenty of outcropping rock in the Midlands and southern England but no evidence for engravings has been found. This suggests that the distribution we see today may be a broadly accurate indication of its distribution in the past. However, it is entirely possible that cup-and-ring designs occurred in different media such as wood carvings or body painting, though no evidence of this has ever been found.

66 Detail of the engravings at Roughtin Lynn - England's largest decorated rock outcrop

...Continued from page 55

organised on the basis of kinship relations and family affiliations but as social networks grew, and the control and exchange of resources became an issue, this social power may have passed to an elite group within society. Whether such power rested in the hands of cult/religious leaders, family elders or tribal councils remains unknown, but there can be no doubt the new power relations resulting from a move to a Neolithic way of life set the course for thousands of years to come.

Further Reading

General
Barber, M., D. Field and P. Topping. 1999. *The Neolithic Flint Mines of England.* Swindon: English Heritage.
Beckensall, S. 1999. *British Prehistoric Rock Art.* Stroud: Tempus.
Bradley, R. 1998. *The Significance of Monuments. On the shaping of human experience in Neolithic and Bronze Age Europe.* London: Routledge.
Bradley, R. 1997. *Rock Art and the Prehistory of Atlantic Europe. Signing the Land.* London: Routledge.
Edmonds, M. 1995. *Stone Tools And Society. Working Stone in Neolithic and Bronze Age Britain.* London: B.T. Batsford.
Gibson, A. and A. Woods, 1997. *Prehistoric Pottery for the Archaeologist.* London: Leicester University Press.
Thomas, J. 1999. *Understanding the Neolithic.* London: Routledge.
Waddington, C. 2004. *The Joy of Flint.* Newcastle: Society of Antiquaries of Newcastle-upon-Tyne.
Whittle, A. 1996. *Europe in the Neolithic. The creation of new worlds.* Cambridge: Cambridge University Press.

Northumberland
Beckensall, S. 2001. *Prehistoric Rock Art in Northumberland.* Tempus: Stroud.
Burgess, C.B. 1990. The Chronology of Cup and Ring Marks in Britain and Ireland. *Northern Archaeology* 10: 21-26.
Gates, T. 1982. A Long Cairn on Dod Hill, Ilderton, Northumberland. *Archaeologia Aeliana* 5th ser. 10: 210-211.
Gibson, A. 1986. Diatom Analysis of Clays and Late Neolithic Pottery from the Milfield Basin, Northumberland. *Proceedings of the Prehistoric Society* 52: 89-103.
Harding, A. 1981. Excavations in the prehistoric ritual complex near Milfield, Northumberland. *Proceedings of the Prehistoric Society* 46: 87-135.
Jobey, G. 1968. Excavations of Cairns at Chatton Sandyford, Northumberland. *Archaeologia Aeliana* 4th series 46: 5-50.
Masters, L. 1984. The Neolithic Long Cairns of Cumbria and Northumberland. In R. Miket and C. Burgess (eds.) *Between And Beyond The Walls: Essays in Honour of George Jobey.* Edinburgh: John Donald: 52-73.
Sockett, E. 1971. Stone axes from Heddon-on-the-Wall. *Archaeologia Aeliana* 4th ser. 49: 240-4.
Tipping, R. 1996. The Neolithic Landscapes of the Cheviot Hills and Hinterland: Palaeoenvironmental Research. *Northern Archaeology* (Special Edition) 13/14: 17-33.
Topping, P. 1997. Different Realities: the Neolithic in the Northumberland Cheviots. In P. Topping (ed.) *Neolithic Landscapes.* Oxford: Oxbow Monograph 86: 113-123.
Waddington, C., K. Blood and J. Crow 1998. Survey and Excavation at Harehaugh Hillfort and Possible Neolithic Enclosure. *Northern Archaeology* 15/16: 87-108.

Waddington, C. 1998. Cup and ring marks in context. *Cambridge Archaeological Journal* 8(1): 29-54.

Waddington, C. 1999. *A Landscape Archaeological Study of the Mesolithic-Neolithic in the Milfield Basin, Northumberland.* Oxford: British Archaeological Reports, British Series 291.

Waddington, C. 2000a. The Neolithic that never happened? In J. Harding and R. Johnston. (eds.) *Northern Pasts.* Oxford: British Archaeological Reports, British Series 302: 33-44

Waddington, C. 2001. Breaking out of the morphological straightjacket: early Neolithic enclosures in northern Britain. *Durham Archaeological Journal* 16: 1-14.

Waddington, C., J. Godfrey and J. Bell. 1998. A chambered tomb on Dour Hill, Northumberland. A detailed survey and re-assessment of the Dour Hill 'long cairn'. *Archaeologia Aeliana* 5th Ser. 26: 1-15.

Waddington, C. and D. Schofield 1999. A new stone-axe source in the Cheviot Hills, Northumberland. *Archaeologia Aeliana* 5th Ser. 27: 175-6.

Waddington, C. and J. Davies 2002. An Early Neolithic Settlement and Late Bronze Age Burial Cairn near Bolam Lake, Northumberland: fieldwalking, excavation and reconstruction. *Archaeologia Aeliana* 5th Ser. 30: 1-47.

5 Later Neolithic and Early Bronze Age

The late Neolithic covers the period from *c.*3200–2500 BC while the early Bronze Age lasts from 2500–1500 BC. The late Neolithic witnesses some important departures from the preceding period, including a change in the type and quantity of ceremonial monuments, as well as changes in pottery styles and lithic technology. In addition, differences in social organisation become increasingly evident, so that by the early Bronze Age there is a greater emphasis on the importance of some individuals within society. At around 2500 BC the first metalwork arrives in Britain and this provides a new medium for the expression of wealth, status and power. It is significant to note that the first metal objects in Britain are usually status objects such as ear-rings, fancy daggers and flat axes. The purely functional tools used for routine tasks do not appear in metal until the end of the early Bronze Age, and as a result flint tools continue to be used throughout.

"Ritual landscapes, megaliths and the dead"

Settlement and Subsistence

67 Infra red aerial image showing details of the Akeld Steads henge

Similar subsistence strategies to those employed during the early Neolithic are thought to have been pursued, with herding, cereal production, hunting, gathering and fishing all still important. Excavated settlement sites dating to this period are few, with the Thirlings site in the Milfield basin remaining the key site in the region. Settlements belonging to the earliest phases of the Bronze Age are rare, although pottery evidence suggests the existence of one near the coast in the area of Ross Links on the north side of Budle Bay, and on the basis of lithic finds another has been suggested at Matfen.

The shift away from a light blade-based technology to a more wasteful flake technology, charac-

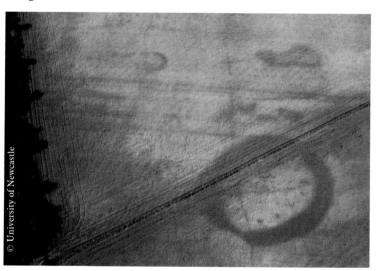

terised by heavier and squat flakes, implies a reduction in settlement mobility as well as a reduced concern for the conservation and maximisation of flint as a raw material. Settlement, it seems, became geared towards an increasingly sedentary pattern for later Neolithic and early Bronze Age groups. Physical remains of early Bronze Age agriculture have recently been recognised in the Cheviots in the Breamish valley. Below the Brough Law hillfort a series of cultivation terraces were identified and subsequent excavation produced early Bronze Age dates for their earliest phase.

The terraces were revetted with low stone walls made from carefully piled clearance stones. The front and rear of the walls had a rough face with the inner core filled with stone rubble. Analysis of the soils showed that they were much thicker than would normally be expected here and that they were stony brown earth soils which would have been very fertile when initial cultivation began. The terracing was evidently constructed to bring more ground into cultivation and to reduce soil erosion. This shows a considerable degree of planning and understanding of the environmental needs of farming.

68 The stone revetment of a cultivation terrace under excavation. Scale = 2m

69 Analysis of the soils suggested cereals had been grown on these terraces

Ritual Landscapes

The late Neolithic witnessed the construction of a wide range of ceremonial monuments, usually of circular form. These included timber circles, stone circles, henges and stone rows, as well as pit alignments, standing stones, ring ditches and cairns. Although the function of stone circles and standing stones remains something of a mystery, these compelling monuments litter the Northumberland landscape, evoking images of ritual, worship, processions, prophecy and, perhaps, sacrifice.

The largest concentration of henge monuments in Britain can be found in the Milfield basin, though these sites are considerably smaller than many of their counterparts in other regions. There are at least eight henge-type monuments in the Milfield area and possibly more. These sites have received considerable attention with excavations carried out by Anthony Harding, Roger Miket and the author (CW).

Other possible henge monuments are known elsewhere in the county, including an unusual enclosure at Ewesley Station north of Scots Gap, a possible site at Alnham and, although covered by a swathe of development, another possible site at Tynemouth.

**70
Northumberland has some fine examples of standing stones such as the circle at Duddo and the cup-marked stone at Matfen**

Cup-and-ring-marked rocks have been found on, and in, these new ritual monuments, suggesting that existing Neolithic traditions were drawn on to sanctify and embellish these new ceremonial centres, while at the same time making explicit linkages with the past. Perhaps this represents an effort to lend the authority of the ancestors to the new religious order?

Continued on page 67...

Case Study: Henges

Henges are circular earthwork monuments formed by an inner ditch and outer mound. As the ditch is situated on the inside the earthworks could not have performed a defensive function. They vary in size from 17m to 427m across, though the average diameter of the Milfield sites is around 25m. Henges usually have a circular setting of standing stones or wooden posts in the central area, creating a sacred space at the heart of the monument. Most have two entrances situated opposite each other, although some of the early henges have only one entrance. Those with opposed entrances are thought to have been designed for inclusion in processional routes across the landscape linking a number of different religious monuments.

© Tim Gates

71 The Coupland henge at over 100m across is the largest in Northumberland

The purpose of henges remains something of a mystery, although in general terms they are widely accepted as being open-air ceremonial centres. We have occasional glimpses of the types of activities that took place inside them as a result of finds made during excavations. At Woodhenge in Wiltshire the remains of a small child with its skull smashed in, probably by a stone axe, was found in a pit. This gruesome act suggests the practice of child sacrifice and, with the body being buried in the monument, it may have served some dedicatory purpose. Although burials are frequently found in henges, they are usually single interments at special places within the monument. Therefore, henges are not usually thought of as cemeteries, since the corpses are considered more likely to have been placed in them as special offerings to empower, or even sanctify, the monument. Some henges have 'coves' situated near the centre of the monument, usually consisting of arrangements of stone slabs. These structures restrict the view of the central area and are thought to have been the focal point for the performance of rituals. Grooved Ware pottery is frequently found at henge sites, and these highly decorated, bucket-shaped vessels are thought to have been directly associated with ceremonial practices. The angular and spiral designs on these ceramics bear similarities with the latest phases of passage-grave art found in the Boyne valley and on Orkney, which some have suggested to be depictions of trance imagery. Quite how these pots were used on henge sites is as yet unclear but it remains possible that they held mind-altering substances for use in rituals. Analysis of residues surviving on pot surfaces from the Balfarg henge complex in Fife has shown that black henbane seeds formed part of the contents. This plant has hallucinogenic properties and it is possible that it may have served some purpose in the henge rituals.

72 The Milfield North Henge

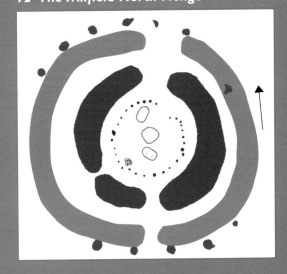

73 Simplified plan of the Milfield North henge

All the henges in the Milfield basin have been flattened and survive only as cropmark sites buried in fields. Based on the evidence from an excavation by Anthony Harding during the 1970's an attempt was made to reconstruct the Milfield North site at the Maelmin Heritage Trail. This site was chosen as it was the most completely excavated and best understood of all the sites. As none of the actual sites are visible above ground it was thought that a full-scale reconstruction would be the best way of visualising a henge and presenting it to the public. The reconstruction was undertaken during April 2000 by a diverse group of volunteers who aimed to construct a 10% portion of the monument using the tools and technology that were available to Neolithic people.

The work included excavating the ditches using antler picks and digging sticks, and scooping up material with shovels made from ox shoulder blades. The post pits were excavated and large timbers set inside them to form a ring of outer posts. A similar ring of 30 smaller posts was set inside the henge. The structural form of the monument was based on the evidence uncovered by the excavations, although the excavator had not been sure at the time whether the inner postholes could have held posts. It was only by building the reconstruction that this could be tested, and the results clearly showed that these smaller holes were capable of holding timber uprights.

74 The recreated henge site under construction

Henges can be found the length and breadth of Britain, from Orkney to Cornwall, and from Ireland to East Anglia. They are an insular British phenomenon, not having continental precursors like earlier enclosures and chambered cairns. The henge phenomenon provides the first evidence for a common cultural tradition that spans all of the British Isles, indicating a sense of cultural, and perhaps religious, unity.

75 The completed reconstruction of the Milfield north henge

...Continued from page 63

Technology

The later Neolithic stone tool manufacturing tradition changed to become less reliant on a blade-based technology with more tools made on squat flakes. Day-to-day tools for practical tasks were often poorly produced, but the prestige pieces that acted as symbols of power, or measures of wealth, were of the highest standards. In fact it is during the late Neolithic and beginning of the early Bronze Age that stone tool manufacture achieved its most sophisticated and elegant forms. These exquisite high-status pieces included arrowheads, chisels, axe-heads, daggers, maceheads, battle axes and carved stone balls.

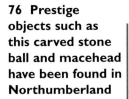

Many of the stone tools dating to this period that have been found in Northumberland are made from high-quality flint that has come from a nodular source. Nodular flint comes from the original geological source, usually within chalk deposits. This flint has few impurities, is often very dark grey or black in colour, and can be recognised by its thin chalky outer crust. It was obtained from properly organised mining operations at sites such as Grime's Graves in Norfolk. Preference for this high-quality mined flint, imported over long distances, suggests exchange routes from Northumberland were extensive and reliable at this time. Furthermore, there existed the capability for moving this heavy and bulky commodity in substantial quantities. Whether this was achieved by sea transport or overland routes remains open to question, but it ensured the inhabitants of Northumberland maintained extensive contacts which must have allowed for the exchange of ideas, beliefs, technology and goods.

76 Prestige objects such as this carved stone ball and macehead have been found in Northumberland

77 This cache of barbed and tanged arrow-heads were found in one of the Milfield North henge pits

As with the stone tool kit, pottery production shows signs of greater specialisation at this time. In the centuries before 3000 BC came the emergence of decorated vessels, usually referred to as 'Impressed Wares' on account of the distinctive impressed patterns often made with the fingertip (sometimes

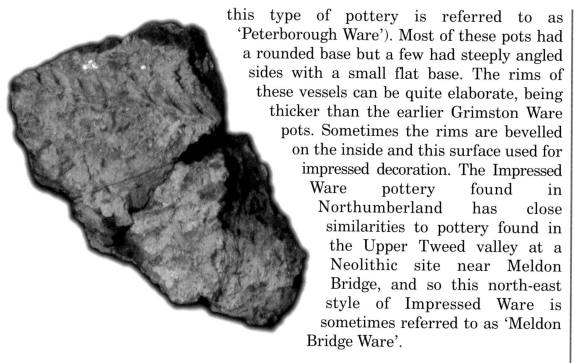

this type of pottery is referred to as 'Peterborough Ware'). Most of these pots had a rounded base but a few had steeply angled sides with a small flat base. The rims of these vessels can be quite elaborate, being thicker than the earlier Grimston Ware pots. Sometimes the rims are bevelled on the inside and this surface used for impressed decoration. The Impressed Ware pottery found in Northumberland has close similarities to pottery found in the Upper Tweed valley at a Neolithic site near Meldon Bridge, and so this north-east style of Impressed Ware is sometimes referred to as 'Meldon Bridge Ware'.

78 Fragmentary sherd of Impressed Ware from Heatherwick, near Elsdon

Slightly later, after 3000 BC, a distinctive type of pottery known as 'Grooved Ware' became widespread across all of the British Isles, often in association with henge monuments. This type of vessel is characterised by its flat base, bucket-shape and all-over decoration that includes parallel lines in the form of grooves or pinched-up lines. The decoration comprises angular designs, such as lozenges, triangles and straight lines, as well as occasional spirals, arranged in geometric patterns. As with henges, Grooved Ware is found all across the British Isles from Orkney to Cornwall and East Anglia to Ireland. It is occasionally found on settlement sites as well, implying that it was not solely for use in the ceremonies that took place in henges. In the Milfield basin Grooved Ware pottery has been found in pits associated with the henge and pit alignment complex at Milfield North and at the henge and ritual complex at Old Yeavering. However, at nearby Thirlings and the southern end of the old airfield near Milfield, Grooved Ware pottery has been found in pits that form part of Neolithic settlement sites. This provides a direct linkage between the settlements and cult centres of the late Neolithic inhabitants in the Milfield basin.

Around 2500 BC a new type of distinctive pottery arrived in the British Isles from the continent. 'Beakers', as they are commonly known, are finely-made pots, assumed to be drinking vessels on account of their shape. They have a thin fabric, bulbous profile, flat base and intricate decoration. The ornamentation of Beakers includes the zoning of decoration by incised lines and the use of fine points to mark the surface. Common designs include lines, dots, zig-zags, cord impressions

79 Grooved ware pottery, such as these sherds from Yeavering, are typically recognised by the use of incised lines

and comb impressions. Beakers have been classified in different ways by archaeologists over the last century according to different criteria such as size, shape and decorative motifs. With the help of radiocarbon dating it is now generally accepted that they can be classified into three basic types according to shape. The earliest of these types is thought to be the 'Bell-Beaker', the second the 'short-necked Beaker', which ultimately gives rise to the third tradition of 'long-necked Beakers'. This general classification appears to work as a rule of thumb but exceptions are known.

80 The earliest form of beakers are 'Bell beakers' such as this one from Rock near Rennington

One of the key questions in prehistoric studies is whether the appearance of Beakers represents the spread of a cultural group, or of an idea, or a mixture of the two. Although archaeologists have furiously debated the 'Beaker question' the evidence remains finely balanced. Beakers are found all over Britain, though many of the early Bell-Beaker forms and their derivatives can be found in eastern areas such as Northumberland, suggesting these were the first areas of contact. According to the first scenario the appearance of this type of pottery is thought to indicate the presence of invaders, and in this way 'pots equal people'. With the second scenario the pots are considered to represent a shared idea that became widespread across western Europe at this time.

It is important to note that early Beakers are most frequently found as grave goods associated with individual burials. Indeed the Beaker forms part of a suite of grave goods that are consistently found together. These include stone wrist guards, jet buttons, thumbnail scrapers, barbed-and-tanged arrowheads and, occasionally, gold ear-rings, button covers, lunulae and bronze daggers. This collection of prestige items is often referred to as the 'Beaker package'. What is perhaps most significant about the arrival of Beakers in Britain is that it is associated with the first metalwork. This consists almost entirely of prestige items such as bronze flat axes and daggers, and ornaments made from gold and silver.

Some archaeologists still argue that the Beaker phenomenon resulted from metal-using invaders arriving from the Continent bringing their own pottery tradition with them. Others, however, see the Beaker package as the accoutrements of a cult that had spread across western Europe at this time. The idea of a cult package has been documented in more recent historical times in the case of the peyote cult that spread from Mexico to Canada. In this case the North American Indians undertook ceremonies that required specific objects including rattles, a carved staff, a feather fan, a small drum and a crescent-shaped altar made from clay or earth. Similarly Beakers may have formed key paraphernalia in ceremonies and public displays by elite members of society. The cult theory gains support when it is considered that there was no associated change in settlement or ceremonial monuments when Beakers arrived, yet this would be expected if invaders had taken over.

However, a shift to the widespread practice of single burials below round mounds does appear to correlate with the presence of beakers. Henges and stone circles continued in use and settlement sites follow the same pattern as before. Still, the fact cannot be escaped that metalwork and Beakers found their way into Britain from the Continent. Recent studies of the oxygen isotope content in human bones from a Beaker burial in Wiltshire suggest some of these people may indeed have come from mainland Europe, and with the increasing use of DNA analysis the question of whether the 'Beaker Folk' really were invaders may yet be fully answered. In the meantime, it seems likely that the answer could be a mixture of the two theories, with the movement of some people, perhaps metalwork specialists (smiths) who brought their knowledge and technology with them, which then became adopted by the native inhabitants. According a high status to smiths is certainly conceivable as the transformation of stone into metal may have been thought of as a magical process.

Around 2000 BC a new type of pottery vessel specifically associated with funerary deposits became widely adopted. Known as 'Food Vessels' since

81 A bi-partite food vessel from a burial near Wooler

82 An enlarged food vessel urn from Goatscrag that contained cremated human remains

the early part of the 20th century, because of their contrast with the drinking-cup form of Beakers, these pots may or may not have actually held food. Food Vessels are found with individual inhumations or cremations, often in stone-lined grave boxes known as cists. Sometimes they occur in the same burial mounds as Beakers, though the Food Vessels are always part of a later, sometimes satellite, insertion. A Food Vessel is a small flowerpot-type vessel usually less than 20cm in height. Larger versions of the same type of pot, more than 20cm in height, are usually referred to as 'Food Vessel Urns' and these can have relief decoration ('Encrusted Urns'). In Northumberland three main types of Food Vessels are found: bipartite, tripartite and bowl-shaped.

Although exhibiting some shared decorative elements with Beakers, such as corded decoration and comb impressions, the closest predecessors to the Food Vessel form are the Neolithic Impressed Wares such as 'Meldon Bridge Ware'. They share the concave neck, decorated heavy rims and, in some cases, the steeply angled body and small flat base. Instead of a curved or flat rim the Food Vessel rims tend to have a bevelled moulding. The decoration ranges from very fine to crudely executed, and makes great use of incised lines and impressed decorative features. Cord decoration, herringbone patterns and chevrons are common motifs. Two finely made vessels from Bolton and Lowick, north Northumberland, are so similar that Alex Gibson has suggested they may have been made by the same potter! The relief decoration on the encrusted Food Vessel Urns tends to be restricted to the neck area between the rim and the shoulder, usually involving chevrons, with the spaces filled with twisted cord or incised patterns.

The precise purpose of Food Vessels remains uncertain but they are thought to have held offerings of food or drink to help the deceased on their journey to the afterlife. As the modern techniques of residue analysis are applied to the contents of these vessels we should learn more about what they once contained and how they were used.

Another type of early Bronze Age pottery, again specifically associated with funerary contexts, is the Cinerary Urn, of which there are two broad types in Northumberland: the 'miniature urn' and the 'urn'. The miniature urns have the same shape and decoration as the larger urns but they tend to be less than 15-18cm in height while the larger ones are usually 20cm or more in height. Urns have been further classified into 'Collared Urns', 'Encrusted Urns', 'Bucket Urns' and so forth, based on variation in shape and form. When found in burial mounds that contain Beaker and Food Vessel burials, urns always occur with the latest burials in the sequence. As with the Food Vessels, Cinerary Urns appear to have developed from the Neolithic Impressed Ware traditions, which already show the use of a collar. Urns are most commonly associated with cremation rites, with many of the Northumberland examples being used to contain the ashes of the dead. More often than not the urn is placed into a mound upside-down with the mouth sometimes sealed by a flat stone or clay plug, although in the case of an urn from Yeavering the ashes were placed in afterwards by breaking the base of the pot when it was set in position. Little is known about the type of people buried in or with urns, though most of the identifiable remains tend to be of women and children.

83 A typical collared urn found near West Hepple

A slightly more unusual form of early Bronze Age pottery is the small vessel type known as 'incense cups'. Although referred to as 'pygmy cups' by Victorian antiquarians on account of their small size, and 'accessory cups' by others, these cups/bowls are usually highly decorated and frequently have perforations in their side walls. The presence of perforations has led

84 An incense cup from Haydon Bridge

Continued on page 77...

Case Study: Bronze

A lthough metal came late to the shores of Britain, it was here that hardened bronze became fully developed by alloying it with tin. Prior to this, much of the continental metalworking had been based around the working of copper and gold, which are soft metals. Bronze is made by combining around 90% copper with 10% tin, though other metals such as arsenic and lead can also be included to enhance certain properties. Copper ores, which occur naturally in mineral-bearing rocks, were mined by battering the rock face with stone mauls, gouging out the softer sediments with bone points and antler picks, and by fire-setting to crack the rock.

85 Stone mauls from Northumberland

The ore, usually malachite or chalcopyrite, was broken down using stone hammers and the copper picked out. It was then smelted with tin until it became molten at 1084° C and poured into a mould. Bronze-casting was used to make a wide variety of implements from weapons to prestige objects.

The earliest bronze objects found in Northumberland are flat axes and, very occasionally, riveted daggers, which date to around 2500 BC. By the middle Bronze Age a wide range of weaponry was in circulation, including spearheads, short swords known as rapiers and dirks, and bronze-covered shields. However, it was not just weaponry that was made from metal: razors, pins, chisels, ear-rings, dress fasteners and even elaborate cups were also made. How far these items were restricted to the wealthy elite or in wider use during the early Bronze Age remains a fascinating question. However, it is clear that the rare gold objects found in some burials, such as ear-rings, cups and capes, were associated with high-status individuals. As time went on, bronze objects became more widely available so that by the middle Bronze Age the use of stone tools had virtually ceased.

86 Socketed axe (middle-late Bronze Age) from Wallington

87 Riveted dagger (early Bronze Age) from Barrasford

Case Study: Howick - Place of the Dead

The 2002 excavations at the Howick Mesolithic site revealed an unsuspected cemetery consisting of five cist graves. 'Cists' are stone-lined grave boxes that were used in Northumberland during the early Bronze Age, c.2000 BC. As the site lay in a ploughed field none of the cists had any surface remains surviving so it is not known whether they originally had mounds above them. None of them had been disturbed by antiquarian excavations or grave robbing, although one had slumped due to its proximity to the cliff edge and another had been disturbed by a later burning pit. The cist boxes were made from sandstone slabs set on end with occasional slabs of mudstone or shale, all of which can be obtained from the cliffs immediately below the site.

88 Excavating the fill from a cist is a painstaking task

Being set into sandy sediments and surrounded by sandstone slabs the cists were in very acidic conditions which meant skeletal remains did not survive. However, cist 2 was an exception because part of the box had been made from Whinstone blocks which is an igneous rock with a slightly alkaline bias. This had created a less acidic environment at one end of the cist and in this area the fragmentary remains of a small skull, that can only have belonged to a very young child, was found. Furthermore, the size of this cist is very small and was evidently designed for an infant.

Immediately on top of the capstone was placed a smoothed limestone cobble that may have been a prototype for a large tool. This piece of rock evidently had significance for the community who buried the child, particularly as further limestone cobbles were associated with some of the other cists. It is likely that the group living at Howick acquired the cobbles from the cliffs below the site. These smoothed cobbles, with fossils visible on their surfaces, may have been thought to have special qualities imbued in them by the gods. If this was the case then such stones may have been recognised as a symbol of ritual power or a talisman for the afterlife.

89 A cist that had a limestone cobble placed on it before and after excavation (Scale: 0.5m)

Of all the five cists only one was of sufficient size for an adult burial, which indicates that the cemetery contained mostly children. This is not all that unusual, as a recently excavated cairn at Turf Knowe in the Breamish valley contained the remains of 22 child cremations. As most people did not receive a special burial in a cist grave this means that the children found in these monuments, and particularly those in single

90 This cist was for an adult burial whereas Fig 89 shows a cist for a small infant (Scale=2m)

graves, must have been of high social ranking. This in turn suggests that by the early Bronze Age status was conferred, at least in part, by lineage. These children appear to have inherited their status from their parents, which means that power and wealth were preserved amongst a social elite that appears to have maintained its position through dynastic lines.

91 A fragment of food vessel from Howick

The only small finds surviving in the acid conditions were some fragmentary pieces of pottery from cist 2 and one small, but carefully decorated sherd from the disturbed area of cist 5. The latter piece of pottery has been adorned with fingernail impressions to create a distinctive herringbone pattern and this allows it to be identified as part of a 'Food Vessel'. It was this small pottery fragment that dated the cists.

The Howick cist cemetery is remarkable for not being located in a prominent position when viewed from the landward side. However, when viewed from the sea it lies on a prominent cliff top on the north side of a small estuary and bay. Antiquarian excavations on a burial mound on the opposite cliff top, to the south of the estuary, revealed another cist burial which contained some human bone fragments and a fragmentary Food Vessel.

Assuming the recently excavated cists had covering mounds this would mean that both sets of graves were visible on either side of the small estuary when approached from the North Sea. This would have sent a powerful visual message to people approaching the inlet, making clear this land already belonged to an elite group whose ancestors were interred there.

92 A food vessel recovered from previous excavations near Howick

...Continued from page 72

archaeologists to think that these small containers may have held incense, or some such substance, for use in ritual practice. They are usually found in burials and some fine examples have been discovered in Northumberland.

Death and Burial

Northumberland has some fine examples of large burial mounds such as the once huge, now partially robbed, cairns above Holystone known as the 'Five Barrows' or the large earthen mounds at Shortflatt and the 'Poind and His Man' near Bolam Lake. The precise date of these large cairns and barrows remains debatable, but they are generally thought to be late Neolithic. These impressive burial mounds appear to have been erected for one, or just a few, individuals, indicating that some members of society were becoming visibly more powerful than others; that is, social stratification was becoming more overt.

93 A Collapsed cist in the 'Football Cairn' on Chirnells Moor, Coquetdale

Burials were frequently accompanied by some of the prestige objects that the individuals had no doubt wielded during their earthly existence or else associated with that individual by the mourners. During the Bronze Age small burial cairns became a very familiar site. Strung out across the moors of Northumberland, and both the Cheviot and sandstone fells, are thousands of stone cairns marking the resting places of Bronze Age people. On the lower ground these burial mounds were sometimes made in earth, though most of them have been ploughed flat by later farming. There are also cases where burials were placed directly into pits cut into the ground, with no evidence for a mound above. The form of these burial monuments varies greatly, even within the same cairn 'cemeteries'. Most of the stone cairns and earthen burial mounds are small, measuring only a few metres in diameter and about half a metre in height. Good examples can be found on Chatton Moor and Sandyford Moor. In the early Bronze Age, 'cist' burials were popular, consisting of stone-lined graves covered by a large capstone with a stone or earth mound raised on top of it. The body was placed inside the cist in a crouched position and sometimes accompanied by grave goods such as a pottery vessel, flint tools and metalwork. Occasionally capstones are found with cup-and-ring marks on them but the markings are always on the underside, facing the corpse.

Another type of cairn is the 'ring cairn', consisting of a circular bank of stones with one or more burials set within the inner area or below the stone bank. Sometimes these banks have a clear entrance through them and sometimes not. Yet another place where early Bronze Age burials have been found is at the foot of rock outcrops, such as at Goatscrag and Corby's Crag, where pots have been discovered containing cremations.

It is not clear whether there was organised religion in the Bronze Age in the way that we would understand it today. However, the widespread use of burial mounds throughout the British Isles and the inclusion of Beakers, Food Vessels and urns, implies that there was a commonly held perception of death and the rituals associated with it at this time. Although there is a great deal of variation in the size, shape and location of burial monuments in the Bronze Age this seems to reflect regional variants of a widely held set of beliefs, rather than the co-existence of separate belief systems.

Burnt Mounds

Burnt mounds are unusual archaeological features that still pose something of a mystery to prehistorians. They consist of circular heaps of burnt stones that usually cover a stone-lined trough and hearth pit and are located close to streams. They were first discovered in Scotland where they are very common, though it was not until recent years that they were realised to have existed across England too. Most of the English examples have been ploughed out but occasional upstanding sites have been recorded. The only site to be excavated in Northumberland is one on Titlington Mount where two out of four mounds were investigated by Pete Topping and the Northumberland Archaeological Group. The radiocarbon dates from the excavation showed that the sites were used over a period extending from around 2000 BC to 1500 BC. Vertical stone slabs, a stone setting and stakeholes were also discovered, indicating that other structural features were associated with the hearths and troughs prior to the mound of burnt stones being piled over them. Burnt mounds are thought to have worked by heating stones in the hearth, placing them into the stone-lined trough and pouring water over them. The water heated up until it gave off steam. The function of these elusive monuments remains hotly debated, with some archaeologists arguing that they were cooking areas, presumably associated with settlement sites, and others arguing that they served as sweatlodges or saunas. At Titlington only two small slivers of bone were discovered and more would be reasonably expected if it were a cooking site. The idea of a sweatlodge is perhaps not too fanciful, as it not only provides an excellent way of cleansing the body and relaxing but may also have served as part of a ritual to purify the body or, through heat exhaustion, to achieve a higher level of consciousness. At one site on Orkney, at a place called Isbister on South Ronaldsway, the burnt mound covered a paved floor that had stone-lined ducts running underneath it that led from the centrally located stone trough. This under-floor central heating, together with the hot water trough, would have certainly caused the interior of the structure to become very warm and damp, which is consistent with the conditions required for a sauna. Could the idea of the Scandinavian Sauna be a relic that has survived from the Bronze Age?

Further Reading

General
Barrett, J. 1994. *Fragments from Antiquity. An Archaeology of Social Life in Britain, 2900-1200BC*. Oxford: Basil Blackwell.
Bradley, R. 1998. *The Significance of Monuments. On the shaping of human experience in Neolithic and Bronze Age Europe*. London: Routledge.
Buckley, V. 1990. *Burnt Offerings: International Contributions to Burnt Mound Archaeology*. Dublin: Wordwell.
Burgess, C. 1980. *The Age of Stonehenge*. London.
Burl, H. A. W. 1976. *The Stone Circles of the British Isles*. New York: Yale University Press.
Burl, H. A. W. 1991. *Prehistoric Henges*. Princes Risborough: Shire.
Edmonds, M. 1995. *Stone Tools And Society. Working Stone in Neolithic and Bronze Age Britain*. London: B.T. Batsford.
Parker-Pearson, M. 1993. *Bronze Age Britain*. London: B.T.Batsford.
Thomas, J. 1999. *Understanding the Neolithic*. London: Routledge.
Tilley, C. 1994. *A Phenomenology of Landscape: Places, Paths and Monuments*. Oxford: Berg.
Topping, P. 2003. *Grime's Graves*. London: English Heritage Guidebook.

Northumberland
Brewis, P. and F. Buckley 1928. Notes on prehistoric pottery and a bronze age pin from Ross Links, Northumberland. *Archaeologia Aeliana* 4th Ser. 5: 13-25.
Burgess, C.B. 1984. The Prehistoric Settlement of Northumberland: A Speculative Survey. In R. Miket and C. Burgess (eds.) *Between And Beyond The Walls: Essays on the Prehistory and History of North Britain in Honour of George Jobey*. Edinburgh: John Donald: 126-175.

Gibson, A. 1978. *Bronze Age Pottery in the North-East of England.* Oxford: British Archaeological Reports, British Series 56.

Harding, A. 1981. Excavations in the prehistoric ritual complex near Milfield, Northumberland. *Proceedings of the Prehistoric Society* 46: 87-135.

Harding, A. 2000. Henge monuments and landscape features in Northern England: monumentality and nature. In A. Ritchie. (ed.) *Neolithic Orkney in its European Context.* Cambridge: McDonald Institute for Archaeological Research: 267-274.

Hewitt, I. and S. Beckensall 1998. The excavation of cairns at Blawearie, Old Bewick, Northumberland. *Proceedings of the Prehistoric Society* 62: 255-274.

Miket, R. 1981. Pit Alignments in the Milfield Basin, and the Excavation of Ewart 1. *Proceedings of the Prehistoric Society* 47: 137-146.

Miket, R. 1985. Ritual Enclosures at Whitton Hill, Northumberland. *Proceedings of the Prehistoric Society* 51: 137-148.

Speak, S. and M. Aylett 1996. The Carved Stone Ball from Hetton, Northumberland. *Northern Archaeology* (Special Edition) 13/14: 179-181.

Stevenson, N. 1998. A possible Neolithic henge monument at Tynemouth, Tyne and Wear. *Northern Archaeology* 15/16: 39-43.

Tait, J. 1965. *Beakers from Northumberland.* Newcastle Upon Tyne: Oriel Press.

Tipping, R. 1996. The Neolithic Landscapes of the Cheviot Hills and Hinterland: Palaeoenvironmental Research. *Northern Archaeology* (Special Edition) 13/14: 17-33.

Topping, P. 1997. Different Realities: the Neolithic in the Northumberland Cheviots. In P. Topping (ed.) *Neolithic Landscapes.* Oxford: Oxbow Monograph 86: 113-123.

Topping, P. 1998. The excavation of burnt mounds at Titlington Mount, north Northumberland, 1992-3. *Northern Archaeology* 15/16: 3-25.

Turner, R. C. 1989. A late Neolithic site at High House, Matfen. *Archaeologia Aeliana* 5th Ser. 17: 215-217.

Waddington, C. 1997. A review of 'pit alignments' and a tentative interpretation of the Milfield complex. *Durham Archaeological Journal* 13: 21-33.

Waddington, C. 1999. *A Landscape Archaeological Study of the Mesolithic-Neolithic in the Milfield Basin, Northumberland.* Oxford: British Archaeological Reports, British Series 291.

Waddington, C. 2003. Threestoneburn Stone Circle, Ilderton, Northumberland *Northern Archaeology* 19: 1-22.

6 Middle and Later Bronze Age

The middle and later Bronze Age was a time of significant change both in the organisation of people's lives and in the way the landscape was used. The ritualised landscapes of the Neolithic and early Bronze Age gave way to a more secular world, where power was in the hands of military elites and the old religious monuments were abandoned. Few ceremonial monuments dating to this period have been found anywhere in the British Isles and the relatively few burials that are known in Northumberland tend to consist of cremations below small stone cairns, or secondary insertions into earlier cairns or barrows. Some recurring ritual acts can be observed in the archaeological record, most notably the preoccupation with burying hoards of metalwork, though not all of these can be considered as ritual deposits. The display of personal wealth and power became important and towards the end of the period the first defended settlements were created. This indicates a rise in social tensions and a need to defend wealth and resources. These Bronze Age groups were devoted almost exclusively to farming, which meant they were anchored to the land and could not simply move on if they were threatened by raiding groups, new settlers or invaders.

"Settled farms and partition of the land"

Settlement

By the middle Bronze Age permanent settlements became widespread and archaeological remains of these structures can be found across Northumberland and elsewhere in England. They consisted of timber-built roundhouses, usually between 6m and 8m in diameter, and the stances for these can be found dotted all over the Cheviot Hills, with a few known on the sandstone hills to the east. Some lower-lying examples are also known, such as the house excavated at Lookout Plantation near Ford. Occasionally some of these houses had stone wall footings, as at Bracken Rigg in Teesdale, but they were otherwise constructed from timber and/or turf. Other variations include those Cheviot sites where clearance stones from surrounding fields were mounded up against the outside walls of timber houses giving the impression, from surface observation, that they were stone-built. However, these 'ring banks' can be recognised as such because they have characteristic low and broad rings of rubble that usually measure in excess of 11m across. Good examples of these 'ring bank' huts have been found during excavations at Green Knowe, Standropp Rigg and Houseledge West.

The function of these circular structures does seem to vary, although they are similar in surface appearance. At Houseledge West, Colin Burgess was able to identify huts that had levelled floors, doorways, porches and roofs as houses, while others, with unprepared floors and clearly not roofed, were seen as stock pens. These huts often occur in groups along the contours of a hillside and are commonly associated with field systems defined by low stone banks and cairns made from stones cleared from the field surfaces. However, as most of the huts were timber-built they leave little or no trace above ground and as a result archaeologists often find the evidence of field systems but are unable to locate the settlements that go with them. Recently two timber roundhouses were discovered by the Northumberland Archaeological Group on a platform on Wether Hill as part of a project to investigate an area between some cairns and a hillfort. These structures were completely invisible from the surface and their remains were only very slight. Taking this into account, and the fact that these unenclosed hut circles extend to the 400m contour, this implies a large population largely devoted to farming. Trying to imagine the barren Cheviot

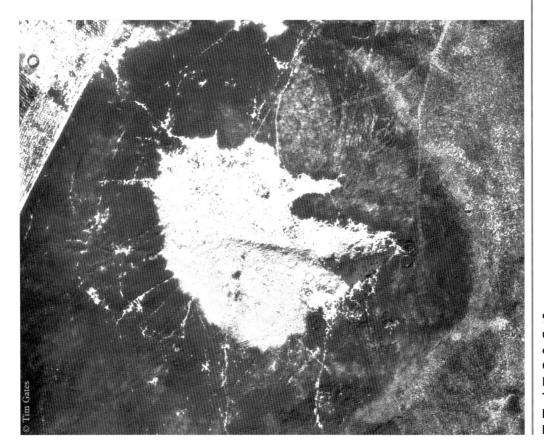

© Tim Gates

94 Bronze Age unenclosed hut circles at Tathy Crags above the Hedgehope Burn. The light patch has formed by the bracken dying off

hillsides of today littered with farms and fields takes a great leap of imagination, but that was indeed the case. Therefore, the population in the middle Bronze Age was probably several times greater than the modern population of the Cheviot valleys.

Evidence for these circular houses is widespread in the uplands of the Borders where they have survived above the limit of medieval and later agriculture. Indeed, the remains on the Cheviot Hills form one of the best-preserved later prehistoric landscapes in Europe with entire settlements and associated field systems surviving intact next to adjoining farm plots of the same age. The layout of these ancient farms can be best seen from the air, and in the right light, crop and soil conditions new sites continue to be discovered. The discovery, recording and survey of this growing number of sites in Northumberland is largely a result of the skilled and painstaking work of Tim Gates who has photographed many of them from the air. Typically these settlements occupy west, east or south-facing slopes, usually positioned on a shelf in the hillside giving way to gently sloping cultivable ground that leads down to a stream. In short, the key factors in site location seem to have been a fairly level surface, sunny aspect, dry ground, proximity to water and cultivable soil. These huts usually occur as single dwellings but can also be found in clusters of half a dozen or more, up to a maximum of twelve.

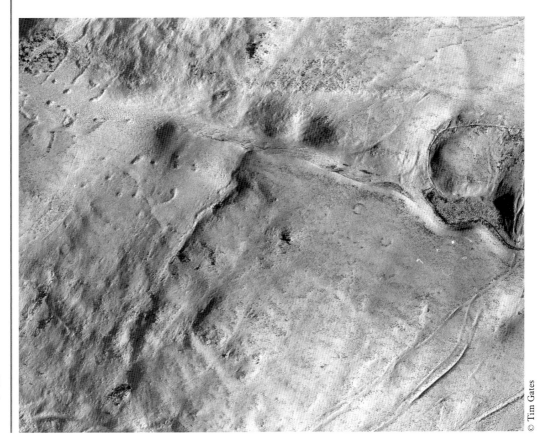

95 Bronze Age huts circles (centre right) and field systems (top left) south of Yeavering Bell

© Tim Gates

Towards the end of the Bronze Age an important new development occurs in the settlement record of the region. Some farms appear to have become enclosed with circuits of timber palisades built to protect them. This move towards enclosure occurs at the end of the Bronze Age, around 800 BC in Northumberland, and is a trend that becomes more pronounced in the succeeding Iron Age. This phase of late Bronze Age enclosure is based on the evidence from excavations by Colin Burgess at Fenton Hill near Doddington. At this site a part-single and part-double palisade was constructed with a single entrance to the west. Other late Bronze Age enclosed sites are known from elsewhere in England, such as Thwing in East Yorkshire and Springfield Lyons in Essex.

96 The earthwork defences of the Fenton Hill enclosure

Subsistence

Analysis of archaeological deposits from the excavated sites in Northumberland has shown that naked and hulled barley were grown, together with emmer and spelt wheat. Occasional hazelnut shells and wild fruit pips have been found but these are much less common than in preceding periods. It was not just foodstuffs that were grown as the Hallshill site, excavated by Tim Gates, produced evidence for the production of flax which can be used both for fabric and oil. The enclosed areas associated with the settlements have been variously termed farmyards, plots, fields and pounds, having an irregular overall plan and sinuous low banks. In some cases lynchets can be observed on the downslope side of these fields, providing further evidence for tilling of the soil. At Houseledge West the presence of pottery fragments, flints and charcoal in the field plots suggests that manuring took place by spreading domestic refuse over them. The plots, though, are generally small, extending over an area of 0.2ha on average.

There is virtually no direct evidence for the type of stock kept by the Bronze Age farmers, largely because the upland soils are now too acid for the survival of bone. However, in lowland and waterlogged settings evidence for Bronze Age animal husbandry should eventually come to light. If Northumberland was not too different from neighbouring regions it can be fairly assumed that sheep, cattle and pig were kept, together with goats and possibly, towards the end of the period, horse.

Metalwork

In the middle and late Bronze Age a wider range of tools and ornaments come into circulation, together with advances in metalworking technology. New types of weaponry that appear in the middle Bronze Age include palstaves (a type of axe), rapiers, dirks, shields and increasingly elaborate spearheads. Towards the end of the 2nd millennium BC dress ornaments become popular, including torcs, finger rings and armbands. By the late Bronze Age a new weapon that denoted the owner as a powerful warrior makes its debut: the sword.

Continued on page 88...

97 Palstave, rapier and side-looped spearhead from Wallington, Blyth and Blagdon respectively

Case Study: Population collapse at the end of the 2nd millennium BC?

A debate has raged amongst archaeologists about whether a settlement collapse occurred in the centuries before 1000 BC. With the exception of the Hallshill site there are no radiocarbon dates from the upland Bronze Age settlements after 1000 BC.

Therefore, it is argued, these farms were abandoned sometime in the late 2nd millennium BC and the population moved down from the high ground, only returning in the Iron Age. Indeed, some archaeologists have gone further and tied this apparent settlement contraction to climatic events caused by the eruption of

98 Lava pool erupting from the earth's core

volcanoes. Colin Burgess has argued that events such as the eruption of Mt. Hekla 3 in Iceland in 1159 BC led to crop failure and ultimately population decline, particularly in marginal areas of the uplands.

This view has been contested by other archaeologists, notably George Jobey, Tim Gates and, most recently, Rob Young, who perceive no dislocation due to the dates from the Hallshill site. This could indeed be the case but it must be noted that Hallshill is only one site and it can be argued that the dates fall into two separate episodes anyway, the second of which may reflect a return to the site in the mid-1st millennium BC after a period of abandonment. Furthermore, the Hallshill site is sometimes termed an 'upland site' but in reality it is located at the bottom range of what can be termed upland lying at just over 229m OD. At this altitude it is not as marginal as the higher upland sites such as Standropp Rigg (380m), Linhope Burn (320m), Houseledge (274m) and Green Knowe (275m), for which the respective radiocarbon dates demonstrate no further activity.

Early 1st millennium dates do exist for lowland sites proper, such as Broxmouth and Dryburn Bridge, and so we are certainly not dealing with total population collapse. The question is really to what extent did settlement contract from the uplands at the end of the 2nd millennium BC before it expanded again in the Iron Age?

The causation issue has tended to revolve around a debate between environmental or social factors. A problem with the volcano theory is that if a population collapse was caused by the eruption of Hekla 3 in 1159 BC then why was there not a similar population collapse after the eruption of Santorini that is dated to 1628 BC? In fact the period of the Santorini explosion in the latter part of the early Bronze Age was a time of population expansion into the uplands. Some may argue that Hekla is nearer to Northumberland than Santorini and that it may, therefore, have had a greater impact. On the other hand, perhaps middle Bronze Age society was less able to cope with such disasters than the more community-based early Bronze Age groups. If it is accepted that there was a contraction of settlement from the uplands in the late Bronze Age then maybe there were other causes, or a combination of causes, of which a volcanic dust cloud was only one.

This debate remains an intriguing area of research for archaeologists and with the availability of new evidence, particularly climatic data from ice cores, the question will continue to be reassessed. In order to broaden the debate we need to acquire more accurate dates from upland and lowland unenclosed settlement sites, together with environmental data relating to the landscapes in which these sites are situated. The environmental information will provide an independent line of enquiry, separate from the archaeological evidence, that will indicate whether agriculture continued at these sites at the time the settlements are thought to be abandoned.

...Continued from page 85

The earliest swords appear in the first centuries of the 1st millennium BC and usually have a leaf-shaped form. Two such swords were discovered in Ewart Park near Wooler in 1814 and have become the type to which most other swords are compared. These two are of particular interest as they had been thrust vertically into the ground. Other examples of this practice are known from elsewhere in the British Isles and it is likely that they reflect an ancient custom, or rite, associated with an emerging warrior elite. Indeed this extraordinary practice has echoes of the Arthurian legend and the drawing of a sword from a stone. Swords are not all that common compared to other forms of weaponry and it is likely that they were very highly prized possessions. It is not difficult to imagine such grand weapons being given names with stories growing up around them and the exploits they were involved in.

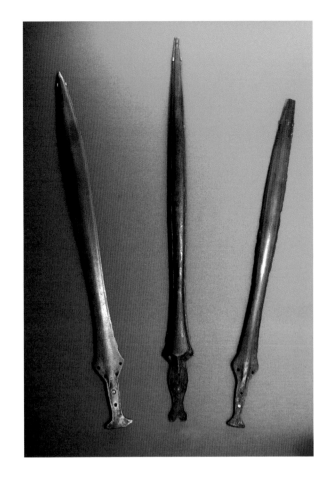

99 Ewart Park type swords from (left to right) Ewart, Newcastle and Glanton

Another piece of armour that appears slightly earlier than the sword is the bronze-covered circular shield, a number of which have been found, particularly in riverine settings. These elegant pieces were made from a single thin sheet of beaten metal, usually with decorative motifs punched from the back. Although beautiful objects these shields would have been virtually useless in combat, indicating that they were for display purposes and a show of strength rather than practical use.

Hoards of metalwork are particularly characteristic of the middle and late Bronze Age and have been found in a wide variety of settings ranging from pits dug into the ground to cave locations and, most commonly, wet places such as lakes, rivers and bogs. Archaeologists have debated the meaning of these hoards for many years, with some arguing that they reflect a strategy for restricting the supply of metal to keep value high, others that the metal was put into safekeeping during times of stress and never recovered, while others have emphasised the votive connotations associated with many of the hoards. It has become increasingly apparent that the majority of metalwork in the British Isles comes from wetland settings, or places that were wet during the Bronze Age. This raises the question of whether this metalwork was

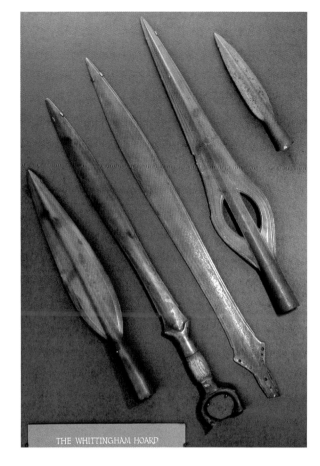

THE WHITTINGHAM HOARD

100 Bronze Age hoards from Wallington and Whittingham

101 A ceremonial bronze shield from Tribley, Chester-le-Street

disposed of in order to demonstrate just how wealthy and powerful someone was, or as part of a ritual act, perhaps to placate the gods. It was a commonly held view in the ancient world that deities inhabited wet places, with springs, pools, waterfalls and bogs also thought of as points of access into the underworld. Given the wide variety of hoards that have been found in many different types of landscape settings it is possible that there are many reasons for the occurrence of Bronze Age hoards, but the argument for their votive connection with watery places is certainly compelling.

Burial

During the middle and later Bronze Age the evidence for burial decreases and it is supposed that bodies were either buried in shallow graves that have left no trace or disposed of in other ways. This may have included burning them and scattering the ashes, or disposal in rivers and wet places together with metalwork. There were fewer new burial cairns constructed but recent excavations uncovered one near Bolam Lake. This site was excavated in order to investigate a Neolithic pottery and stone tool scatter that was found on the field surface. It was a surprise, then, when a low stone cairn was revealed after the first cut by the digger. In fact, the appearance of a cairn on this spot was even more staggering as it had produced a reaction in the dowsing rods being used by the author (CW) to position the excavation trench!

102 Members of the Northumberland Archaeological Group uncovering a newly discovered burial cairn near Bolam Lake

The cairn consisted of a low circular stone mound measuring 4m in diameter and up to 0.3m high at its centre. Below the cairn three pits had been dug and cremations of separate individuals placed in each. These included the remains of three adults of indeterminate age, one of whom was a female. The evidence for warping and cracking of the long bones indicates that the bodies were cremated 'fleshed'. Also, some green staining of the bones suggest that copper alloy objects, probably dress fastenings, may have accompanied the bodies during burning. When the cairn was raised over the pits the remains of cremated animals appear to have been thrown on to it. A radiocarbon determination of c.900 BC was obtained from a charred twig within one of the cremation deposits, providing a secure late Bronze Age date. Whether the people under this cairn were related remains unknown but it certainly has the feel of a family burial. No grave goods were found associated with the burials which, together with the preference for cremation, demonstrates a departure from earlier burial practices. The burnt remains of these people were reburied in the same part of the field once the analysis was complete.

103 The burial cairn after being half-sectioned

Further Reading

General
Barrett, J. 1994. *Fragments from Antiquity. An Archaeology of Social Life in Britain, 2900-1200BC.* Oxford: Basil Blackwell.
Bradley, R. 1990. *The Passage of Arms. An Archaeological Analysis of Prehistoric Hoards and Votive Deposits.* Cambridge: Cambridge University Press.
Burgess, C. 1980. *The Age of Stonehenge.* London. J.M. Dent & Sons Ltd.
Cowie, T.G. and Shepherd, I.A.G. 2003. The Bronze Age. In Edwards, K.J. and Ralston, B.M. (eds.) *Scotland After the Ice Age.* Edinburgh: Edinburgh University Press: 151-168.
Parker-Pearson, M. 1993. *Bronze Age Britain.* London: B.T.Batsford.

Northumberland
Burgess, C. 1968. *Bronze Age Metalwork in Northern England c.1000 to 700B.C.* Newcastle Upon Tyne: Oriel Press.
Burgess, C. 1984. The Prehistoric Settlement of Northumberland: A Speculative Survey. In R. Miket and C. Burgess (eds.) *Between And Beyond The Walls: Essays on the Prehistory and History of North Britain in Honour of George Jobey.* Edinburgh: John Donald: 126-175.
Burgess, C. 1985. Population, Climate and Upland Settlement. In D. Spratt and C. Burgess (eds.) *Upland Settlement in Britain. The Second Millenium B.C. and after.* Oxford: British Archaeological Reports 143: 195-230.

Burgess, C. 1990. Discontinuity and Dislocation in Later Prehistoric Settlement: Some Evidence From Atlantic Europe. *Colloque International de Lons-le-Saunier* 16-19 mai: 21-40.

Burgess, C. 1980b. Excavations at Houseledge, Black Law, Northumberland, 1979, and their implications for earlier Bronze Age settlement in the Cheviots. *Northern Archaeology* 1(1): 5-12.

Burgess, C. 1989. Volcanoes, catastrophes and the global crisis of the late second millenium. *Current Archaeology* 10: 325-9.

Cowen, J. D. 1933. Two bronze swords from Ewart Park, Wooler. *Archaeologia Aeliana* 4th Ser. 10: 185-198.

Gates, T. 1983. Unenclosed Settlements in Northumberland. In J. C. Chapman and R. H. Mytum (eds.) *Settlement in North Britain, 1000B.C.-1000A.D.* Oxford: British Archaeological Reports 118: 103-48.

Jobey, G. 1980. Green Knowe unenclosed platform settlement and Harehope cairn, Peebleshire. *Proceedings Society of Antiquaries of Scotland* 110: 72-113.

Jobey, G. 1983. Excavation of an unenclosed settlement on Standropp Rigg, Northumberland, and some problems related to similar settlements between Tyne and Forth. *Archaeologia Aeliana* 5th ser. 11: 1-21.

Jobey, G. 1985. The Unenclosed Settlements of Tyne-Forth: A Summary. In D. Spratt and C. Burgess (eds.) *Upland Settlement in Britain. The Second Millenium B.C. and after.* Oxford: British Archaeological Reports 143: 177-194.

Young, R. and T. Simmonds 1995. Marginality and the nature of later prehistoric upland settlement in the north of England. *Landscape History* 17: 5-16.

Waddington, C. and J. Davies 2002. Excavation of a Neolithic settlement and late Bronze Age burial cairn near Bolam Lake, Northumberland. *Archaeologia Aeliana* 5th series, 30: 1-47.

7 | Iron Age

The Iron Age is often considered synonymous with the 'Celts', conjuring a romantic image of druids, bards, warriors, princesses and the stuff of legends. However, it was only at the beginning of the 18th century that the term 'Celtic' came to be applied to the Welsh, Irish, Scots and Bretons. This came about as a direct result of a text by a Welsh scholar, Edward Lhuyd, who advanced the view that the Welsh, Breton, Irish and Gaelic languages were all related to ancient Gaulish and decided to collectively label these languages 'Celtic'. This provided an artificial sense that the people who inhabited the British Isles were Celts like those on the Continent. If we look to the writings of the Greco-Roman world, where the term 'Celt' comes from, it is manifestly clear that the various writers only ever refer to continental peoples as 'Celts', often as another word for 'Gaul', but never to describe the British or Irish. Indeed, Caesar treated Gauls and Britons as ethnically different and records that the British tribes considered themselves indigenous. The Romans also noticed ethnic differences between the various inhabitants of the British Isles and used the name 'Brittones' for people in the north and 'Britanni' for those in the south. So although Britain still has strong traditions stretching back to the Iron Age they are not strictly speaking 'Celtic', but rather indigenous traditions that should be called by another name. The Roman name for our island was 'Britannia', which meant 'land of the Britons', and therefore it is probably most appropriate to call our indigenous Iron Age traditions 'British' or 'Brittonic'. Next time you buy a piece of 'Celtic' jewellery think of it instead as 'British' jewellery.

"Hillforts and Britons"

This is not to say that the Iron Age British did not have customs, beliefs and linguistic elements in common with their Gaulish neighbours. A good example of shared customs was Druidism. Caesar wrote in Book VI of his 'Gallic Wars' that,

"It is thought that this [Druidic] system of training was invented in Britain and taken over from there to Gaul, and at the present time diligent students of the matter mostly travel there to study it."

So it is evident that although ethnically separate, the Iron Age British maintained close contacts with their continental neighbours.

Settlement

The settlement record for the Northumbrian Iron Age is usually thought to consist of hillforts, hillforts and more hillforts. But such a view does not adequately account for the breadth of settlement types that we now know about. Unenclosed settlements, often grouped in clusters and rebuilt over time, have been discovered recently at Pegswood near Morpeth and further north at Chevington. These small villages were almost certainly farming settlements and consisted of closely spaced timber-built round-houses. Another unenclosed settlement has also been discovered below the Roman fort at South Shields and this had two phases of cultivation plots associated with it. The main cereals grown here were spelt wheat and hulled barley, remains of which were found inside a roundhouse. Some iron tools were also preserved in the roundhouse, including an adze that had been buried in a pit, together with a ring-headed pin, rods and a punched metal strip. The roundhouse was dated to the middle Iron Age, sometime in the period 390-170 BC, and together with the two sites mentioned earlier, this evidence has overturned the previous view held by some archaeologists that enclosed settlements predominated in the north-east at this time. Interestingly the South Shields house had been deliberately burnt down and abandoned before the area was used for agriculture later in the Iron Age. Whether this was an aggressive act or part of a ritualised 'closing' of the site, perhaps after the inhabitants had died, remains uncertain.

Continued on page 100...

104 This Iron Age round house was discovered below the Roman fort at South Shields

Case Study: Roundhouses and The Brigantium House

A popular reconstruction from prehistory is the roundhouse, a number of which can be seen around the country today at places such as Butser Hill in Hampshire and Castell Henllys in Pembrokshire.

It had long been thought that in Northumberland roundhouse walls were built from timber during the Bronze and Iron Age and only in the Roman period were they built in stone. However, recent excavation evidence from a palisaded site at Fawdon Dean in the Cheviots (see below) has produced Iron Age dates for stone-built round-houses with paved floors.

At Brigantium, in Redesdale, a stone-built roundhouse has been reconstructed, based on an excavated site at nearby Woolaw Farm, 1.5km away (see figure 120). This roundhouse was located inside a rectangular enclosure which is likely to be of Romano-British date. The roundhouse was constructed as an experiment and is currently the only stone-built roundhouse in Britain.

105 The dry-stone walls of the Brigantium roundhouse under construction

The sloping ground had first to be levelled off and the position of the roundhouse marked out. The hut had an external diameter of 11m with walls 1m wide at their base. The drystone walls were constructed first by professional wallers using the local sandstone. They were built with facing stones to the front and back and a rubble core between, as had been revealed by the original excavation. The interior paving was then laid and a hearth set in the centre.

Once the walls had been completed a timber collar made from ash was laid along the top of the wall and fastened together using wooden pegs. This was necessary in order to spread the weight of the roof along the walls and prevent the roof timbers from toppling it. This ring beam also served to convert the outward push of the roof into a vertical push, thus stabilising the walls. Once the ring beam was secure, three of the timber roof poles were tied together at one end on the ground and then lifted up and secured against the ring beam so that the tied end formed the apex of a conical roof. Additional roofing timbers were then added to form the roof frame characteristic of all roundhouses.

Once the roof timbers were in place, a lattice-work of hazel and willow rods was tied across the roofing poles to form spars on to which thatch could be tied. A plant-fibre cord was used to secure the spars as this type of twine is known to have been used in the Iron Age. Once the spars were in place bundles of straw thatch were tied on to the roof. The thatch was attached in consecutive rings, starting at the eaves of the roof then working upwards towards the apex. Once the roof was in place a timber frame for a door was put in place, again based on the evidence from the excavated site.

Evidence for interior wattle and daub had been found at the Woolaw site so it was decided to experiment by daubing half of the inside wall of the roundhouse. Timber hurdles made from coppiced hazel and alder were secured against the wall with wooden pegs and cord. Then a mixture of clay, straw and water was prepared and applied to the hurdles, which provided a bonding surface in the same way as laths do today. When it dried this daub served to render the internal wall making it draught-proof. However, with time the daub cracked as the clay dried out, suggesting that more straw, sand or dung should have been added to the mixture to reduce the effects of shrinkage. However, smearing a slip of daub over the surface has helped to fill the cracks. Other benefits of this plastered interior are that it reflects heat from the fire, keeping the inside warmer, and when painted white it also reflects light, making the interior brighter.

The Brigantium roundhouse has proved very popular with the public but some mysteries still remain. Originally the hut was constructed without a smoke hole in the roof. However, when a fire is lit the hut fills with smoke that is potentially carcinogenic and takes time for people to get used to, if they ever do. Some argue that the smoke would have percolated through the thatch and in so doing drive out vermin and keep the roof dry. Others think that the type of wood being burnt would have been specially selected so that the fire was virtually smokeless. Others, however, believe that a smoke hole would have been used that could be opened or closed to release smoke and control the fire.

107 The Brigantium round house after completion

Case Study: Fawdon Dean

On the flanks of Wether Hill, overlooking the deeply incised Fawdon Dean, near Ingram, the cropmarks of two overlapping enclosures were identified as a result of aerial reconnaissance. As part of a Northumberland National Park and University of Durham project the sites were investigated in collaboration with the author (CW). Although there was little trace of any remains above ground, once excavation began it became clear that there were some extremely well-preserved remains below the surface.

© Tim Gates

108 The Fawden Dean enclosures were discovered by aerial photography

109 The remains of a stone built roundhouse begin to emerge

The excavation demonstrated that the smaller enclosure was earlier and dated to the late Iron Age, whereas the larger enclosure that cut it belonged to the early Romano-British period. As excavations in the earlier enclosure proceeded, the remains of stone-built roundhouses were discovered set into scoops cut into the hillside. The floor of one hut had been paved but the ditch of the second enclosure cut right through the middle of it.

110 Remains of a roundhouse with the later enclosure ditch running through

111 A second roundhouse emerges in the later enclosure

The interior of the later enclosure was not as well preserved, although the arc of one stone roundhouse wall did survive, together with some occupation deposits, flagging and internal pits that had been protected by the wall tumble. Radiocarbon dates from the construction phase of the roundhouse wall indicated a Romano-British date. A large quernstone for grinding wheat was found wedged into one of the pits inside this roundhouse. Elsewhere in the enclosure were the remains of charcoal pits, one of which had a copper alloy object and a Roman coin associated with it, suggesting that metalworking may have taken place on the site.

Excavation across the enclosure circuit revealed ditches with near-vertical sides and evidence for timber posts surviving in some sections. Elsewhere along their circuits the ditches become wider than would normally be expected for a palisade trench, but they still remain nowhere near as wide as the defensive ditches found on other enclosed sites. Therefore, the exact form of these palisade-style enclosures remains frustratingly vague, but there were clearly timber defensive works on these hillside sites.

...Continued from page 94

Palisades

Palisaded enclosures, that is sites defended by a wooden stockade, have a long chronology in Northumberland and the Borders, with examples known from late Bronze Age through Iron Age to Romano-British times. The distribution of palisaded settlements shows sites in both upland and lowland situations. Some of them, such as Dod Law West (phase 1), Horsedean Plantation and Ingram Hill, occur in isolation, while others are located in pairs, such as those at Hetton Hall and Alnham. Whether these latter sites represent a cumulative sequence of occupation, as is the case with the superimposed palisades at Fawdon Dean, or contemporary settlements near to each other, remains unknown. Generally the pattern seems to be one of a patchwork of self-contained fortified farmsteads dispersed across the landscape, each with access to a variety of soils, terrain types and a water source. The practice of mixed farming appears to have been undertaken and considerable inroads into the woodland cover must have been made to obtain the large quantities of timber necessary to build these settlements. The need to build defended settlements around this time indicates increased stress within society and a period of social instability and insecurity.

© Tim Gates

112 The unusual double enclosures at Old Bewick hillfort

Hillforts and Territory

Perhaps the most easily recognised and ubiquitous prehistoric monument to be found in Northumberland is the hillfort. Indeed the county is home to the largest concentration of these sites anywhere in England. The Northumbrian hillforts differ somewhat from their counterparts in the south, such as those of Wessex, as they are generally quite small. Some of these hillforts could be characterised as fortified farmsteads since many are of the same size as the earlier palisaded sites that sometimes underlie them, as at Ingram Hill and possibly Witchy Neuk.

113 Section of surviving wall face at Humbleton Hill

They were probably home to extended farming families, numbering between 30 and 100 people depending on the size and number of huts. Although small, the defences on these sites are often substantial and well made, serving not only a defensive function but also as an ostentatious statement of prestige and power. Indeed, gateways and the ramparts on the main approach to a hillfort frequently display greater elaboration and greater height than on other parts of the defensive circuit, as at Harehaugh and Lordenshaws, for example. Although these defences are usually visible on the ground as grass-covered banks and ditches many of the forts had stone-faced ramparts with rock-cut

ditches to the front, the latter having usually silted up. In some cases
the defences consist of a single perimeter of bank and ditch, as at
Howick Burn, Witchy Neuk or Great Wanney, or a single stone wall,
as at Greaves Ash and West Sinkside, and these are termed 'unival-
late'. In other cases, such as at Great Hetha and Colwell Hill, they
may have two circuits of defences (termed 'bivallate'), or more than
two, such as Castle Hill and Ring Chesters ('multivallate'). Sometimes
fort defences are more complex, having two or three circuits on their
weakest side and only one around the rest of the circuit, as at
Harehaugh for example. Such forts, therefore, have part-univallate
and part-multivallate defences. The low bank that is sometimes found
just beyond the outer lip of the ditch is known as the 'counterscarp'
and was probably there to prevent people and animals from coming
too close to the ditch edge.

Ditches are typically around 2.5m deep and have a v-shaped profile,
while the ramparts are thought to have stood between 1.5m and 3m
high, with some surmounted by a timber breastwork. The hillfort
builders were not content with just providing defences, though; they
applied their understanding of terrain to select the most advantageous
positions. As the name suggests, hillforts usually, though not always,
occupy hilltop positions with commanding views. They are typically
located with steeply sloping ground leading up to them, which would

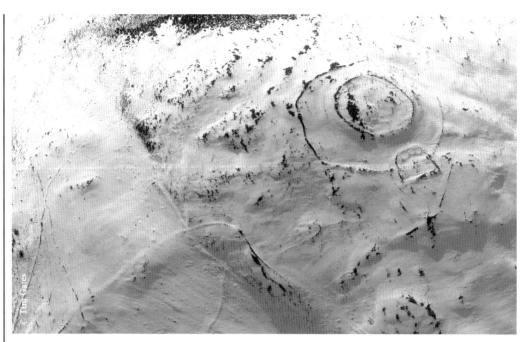

115 The Iron Age hillfort on West Hills, Kirknewton, under a snow cover. A Romano-British rectinlinear settlement with hut circles can be seen overlying the outer rampart

help take the sting out of an attack and reduce the chance of a surprise assault. Classic examples of these hilltop sites include West Hills above Kirknewton, Brough Law in the Breamish valley and Ros Castle above Chillingham. When visiting hillfort sites you will regularly see precipitous slopes deliberately incorporated into the defensive circuit. Good examples of this can be seen at Middle Dean in the Breamish valley, Humbleton Hill west of Wooler, and Harehope camp to the east of Old Bewick. Elsewhere you can find defences positioned on rising ground so that each successive rampart sits higher than the one before it, as in the case of the western defences at Harehaugh Hillfort.

116 The remains of a buried hillfort containing round houses near Marleyknowe, Milfield, visible as crop marks

117 This hillfort south of Howick is an example of a coastal fort overlooking a small estuary

Hillforts are not exclusive to the high ground of Northumberland but can also be found in the lowlands and on the coastal plain. Aerial reconnaissance around the Milfield basin has identified a whole series of lowland hillfort sites in what is now agricultural land. The massive ditches of these sites have been filled in, presumably with the rampart material, and years of subsequent ploughing has meant these sites are invisible on the ground. So far none of these sites have been investigated by excavation and it remains an important research priority to understand them and test whether they are contemporary with, and of similar character to, the more visible upland sites.

Out towards the coast a number of enclosed sites and hillforts proper can be found where farming has not altogether obliterated their remains. One of the best-preserved sites is the hillfort at Howick which occupies a steep-sided bluff above a small estuary. Sections of stone-faced rampart can still be seen at this site and in 1817 sword fragments and Roman coins were found when the interior of the site was ploughed up. Elsewhere along the coast Iron Age enclosures are known on Howick Scar, on Scrog Hill next to Dunstanburgh Castle, and at Warren Mill and Easington near Budle Bay. An Iron Age fort is also thought to have existed below Bamburgh Castle, which occupies a strong natural position on a steep-sided rock outcrop.

Although dominated by these smaller forts Northumberland does have a number of much larger sites that compare directly with the southern hillforts. In particular these include the sites at Yeavering Bell, Humbleton Hill, The Kettles and a new site that has been discovered partly overlain by Norham Castle. These sites are considerably larger than most of the other forts and at Yeavering, where the defences enclose an area of over 5ha, there is evidence for at least 130 huts, indicating a once-thriving town on this unlikely windswept perch. All these circular huts were made of timber and this is nearly always the case at hillfort sites. Yeavering Bell is an altogether impressive site, being the most prominent of the northern ring of Cheviot Hills and with conspicuous twin peaks. It commands wide views out over the breadbasket that was the Milfield basin and further north towards the Merse, while to the east the North Sea can also be seen on a fine day. The site controls access up the Glen valley, which provides one of the few east-west routes across the country, making it an important strategic routeway throughout history. The defences consist of a single drystone wall rampart, that has now largely collapsed, with a small annexe at each of the east and west ends. Although not excavated in recent years, earlier finds from the site suggest occupation lasting from the Iron Age into the Roman period, when it appears to have still served as a tribal centre for the Votadini tribe.

118 The largest hillfort in Northumberland is that pictured here on Yeavering Bell. It contains remains of at least 130 hut platforms

© Tim Gates

Such continuity into the Roman period is rare, as most hillforts either go out of use at the end of the Iron Age or display a different pattern of occupation. Where occupation continues, the defences have usually been largely flattened, or at least abandoned, and new unenclosed settlements consisting of stone-built roundhouses built over them. In some cases the roundhouses actually sit on top of the levelled Iron Age ramparts. Good examples of this later use of hillfort sites can be seen at Warden Law above the confluence of the two Tynes, and at Wether Hill in the Breamish valley. Quite why most hillforts were taken out of commission as defended sites remains conjectural but it is likely that, whatever agreement the Votadini tribe came to with their Roman neighbours to the south, one of the conditions was the demilitarisation of some of their settlements.

Rectilinear Hillforts and Enclosures

There are two examples of upland rectilinear 'hillfort' sites, thought to be Iron Age in origin, currently known in Northumberland; one is the site at Manside Cross near Elsdon and the other a site on Ewesley Fell to the north of Scots Gap. A further site may exist at High Rochester in Redesdale where geophysical survey has suggested the existence of a similar buried enclosure. The date of these sites has not yet been determined but trial excavations by George Jobey at Manside Cross showed that it was certainly occupied in Roman times. In the lowlands, cropmark sites of Iron Age enclosures have been recognised at Hazlerigg, Winlaton Mill, Scremerston, Hartburn, Burradon and at West Brandon and West House in County Durham. The sites at

Hartburn, Burradon and Apperley Dene have significantly smaller inner enclosures that date to the Roman period, set within larger outer enclosures which represent an earlier, presumably prehistoric, phase. More radiocarbon dates are required from these various rectilinear sites if their chronology is to be more thoroughly understood.

Another form of enclosure that is common in Northumberland, particularly in the south-west close to the Roman supply route of Dere Street, is the smaller 'rectilinear enclosure'. These consist of a single or double bank and ditch with one or two entrances, enclosing an area usually less than 0.2ha. They have very regular outlines and the upstanding ones in the valleys of the Rede and North Tyne are usually stone-built, although they appear now as grass-covered mounds. Stone hut circles and sunken yards can often be discerned inside these enclosures which are widely regarded as farming settlements belonging to the Roman period. However, a campaign of excavations at a number of these sites by George Jobey has revealed that some of them had Iron Age origins. In some cases stone huts had been built over earlier timber-built huts, and radiocarbon dates from Belling Law and Kennel Hall Knowe show some of these timber huts to be late Iron Age. At sites such as Kennel Hall Knowe and Tower Knowe the later banks had been built over earlier wooden stockades. However, it is important to note that the

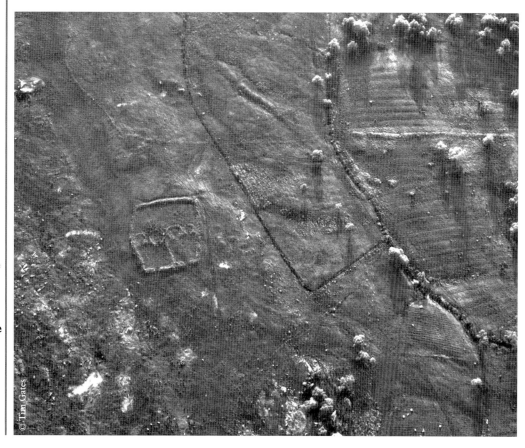

120 A rectilinear Romano-British site at Woolaw, Redesdale, (centre left) with associated cord rigg cultivation (bottom right). The broader medieval ridge and furrow can be clearly seen to the right of the pin-stripe patch of cord rigg

© Tim Gates

construction stages of the enclosure banks themselves have not yet revealed evidence for a pre-Roman date and, therefore, the question remains as to whether the rectilinear enclosures themselves go back to the Iron Age or represent a widespread remodelling of existing sites into a new form during the early Roman period? If the latter, then they represent a new type of 'model' farm that would appear to be introduced and not an indigenous development. It is a salient point that none of the rectilinear enclosures have produced evidence of use after about the 2nd century AD, suggesting that they may have been part of a short-lived Roman policy exercised when Roman control extended north into Scotland.

Another question relating to these sites is also of interest. In the past archaeologists have viewed them as settlements without any defensive purpose, based on the assumption that the encircling banks were always low. In these cases the enclosure is thought to have only existed to form a stock-yard, or as a way of defining the homestead itself and making a statement of ownership. The wall bases are usually 1.5m wide with a built face front and back, and a core consisting of rubble and clay. An experimental reconstruction at the Brigantium Centre in Redesdale has shown that a 3.5m high drystone wall can be built on a 1.5m base and that it is still wide enough at the top to build it higher, or to place a stout timber breastwork on top. It was found that once the clay had settled, it bound the wall and timbers together very tightly, making it a considerable defensive barrier. Although this does not prove that these enclosures were defensive it raises the question whether some of them were constructed with defence in mind. If this were the case, it would support the view for planned farmsteads imposed under Roman control. It is likely that the inhabitants of these farms were native British as very little in the way of Roman finds have been discovered on these sites. Whether they were Britons indigenous to the area or brought in from other regions remains unknown. It is also noteworthy that in Redesdale, North Tynedale and the Milfield basin these enclosures are spaced close to the main Roman roads leading northwards and set at regular intervals on the springline. They clearly reflect a planned settlement pattern of some sort.

Subsistence

It is widely thought that the Iron Age inhabitants of Northumberland were, in the main, mixed farming groups. Due to the acid soils, little in the way of animal bone survives but occasional fragments of bone and teeth belonging to cattle, sheep and horse have been found. Barley, wheat, oats and flax were grown in the fields surrounding settlement and defended sites. In fact the remains of some of these agricultural plots can still be recognised in upland areas where the narrow ridges still survive from the last harvest. These ridges, with slight furrows between, occur in long strips, giving the ground a striped appearance. The ridges are usually set between 1m and 2m apart and are referred to by archaeologists as 'cord rigg', as it is much narrower than the more familiar 'ridge and furrow' of the medieval period. The reason for the riggs being narrow may be that they were hand-dug, in the same way perhaps as 'lazy-bed' agriculture. However, further investigation of these agricultural relics may reveal the use of ards or ploughs in the formation of the riggs. The grain produced from these crops was used to make flour which could be turned into staples such as bread, together with malted barley used to make beer and oatmeal for porridge. The stalks and chaff were probably collected and used as animal feed over the winter.

It has long been asked whether all the hillforts are contemporary or whether they represent different phases of occupation. Recent results from excavations on sites in the Breamish valley lend support to the view that many were occupied at the same time. With evidence for long, low, walled boundaries between the different hillfort blocks this suggests that each hillfort had a defined 'territory' around it. In the case of the Breamish valley the sites at Brough Law, Middle Dean and Wether Hill would each have had access to the river along with an area of valley floor, valley side and upland. By dividing the landscape equally, each group got access to areas of meadow, agriculture, grazing and, presumably, woodland. What is more, in times of failed crop or flooding it would mean that each group was insured against famine by not being over-reliant on one area of the landscape, or one type of foodstuff. Perhaps this is another reason why the Iron Age forts formed centres for mixed farming production.

121 Saddle quern with rubbing stone from Colwell.

Tools and Technology

The Iron Age heralded the introduction of innovations, not least of which was the use of iron for making tools, weapons, armour and bindings. Greater technological expertise was required to smelt iron, due to its high melting point (1545°C), but it offered significant advantages over bronze, including greater strength and the almost ubiquitous availability of iron ore. Unlike iron ore, copper deposits are rare which meant that during the Bronze Age the supply of copper could be strictly controlled by certain groups who would have no doubt acquired considerable wealth in the process. With the introduction of iron technology all this changed, as virtually every region had access to iron deposits. This would have had an important impact on restructuring the balance of power between different tribes.

With the ready availability of iron a much wider range, and greater abundance, of metal objects came into use, particularly by the late Iron Age. This included all sorts of things from buckets and mirrors to cauldrons and fire dogs. Indeed all the basic woodworking tools with which we are familiar today were present during the Iron Age, and the availability of these tools allowed further innovations to take place. Chariots and carts became more widely used and horse harnesses are a common find, reflecting the importance of the horse as a prestigious symbol of the British warrior class. Bronze artefacts continued to be made though, especially for intricate cast pieces such as brooches, fibulae, tankard handles, rings and bindings.

The Iron Age pottery of Northumberland is usually rather hard to identify but recent finds from sites at Dod Law West, Fawdon Dean and elsewhere have shown that large bucket and barrel-shaped vessels predominated. These were almost certainly used as storage containers, though some pots were used for cooking, and others, such as flagons, for drinking – a notorious habit of the Britons noted by Roman writers! During the late Iron Age the technology to produce finer wheelthrown pottery was introduced into southern areas of Britain but this technology did not reach Northumberland until the arrival of the Romans, around 79 AD.

Social Organisation

The large number of hillforts and related sites known in the county, between 150 and 200, suggests that groups were somewhat independent and keen to guard their small tightly-knit community. Perhaps a clan-based structure can be envisaged where each extended family group stridently maintained its independence from its neighbours. The presence of a few large hillforts, though, does suggest these small independent-minded groups may have recognised affinities with a larger tribal grouping. Indeed, by the end of the Iron Age there was a collective name for the tribe inhabiting the eastern side of Northumberland, at least as far south as the Coquet. They were known to the Romans as the 'Votadini', while those in Tynedale are thought to have belonged to the great northern federation known as the 'Brigantes'.

It is not just the archaeological remains that provide our understanding of Iron Age society, as the Roman writers have left us with a variety of informative accounts about the Britons and their Celtic continental cousins. In late Iron Age society class distinction appears to have been very marked. Warring tribes would raid each other to gather slaves who could be exported to the Continent in exchange for exotic goods, precious metals and so forth. Strabo stated that the main exports from Britain were corn, hunting dogs, tin and slaves! Most people were farmers and would have been engaged in the daily toil of animal husbandry and crop production, but in times of stress it is likely they would have been called on to fight and so are likely to have been familiar with the ways of war. However, it was a warrior aristocracy that controlled society, and this could include female as well as male rulers. In addition to the farmers and aristocracy was a wide spectrum of artisans including metalworkers, carpenters, boat makers and so forth. But the most intriguing group has to be the druids, the priestly class who held great sway over all society, including the aristocracy.

The Romans describe the druids as religious leaders, judges, philosophers, healers, magicians, astronomers, mathematicians and prophets. They seem to have enjoyed a unique status both in Britain and beyond and were written about in admiring terms by early Christian residents of Alexandria, Egypt, although it is unlikely any of these writers ever met druids. Caesar wrote that the druids would study for up to 20 years, that they did not pay taxes as was customary for the rest of society, and that they thought it improper to commit their studies to writing. Both men and women could be druids and people could apparently join of their own accord. The druids undertook much of their training in secret and sacred places, with caves and secluded groves mentioned as being typical. As keepers of the oral tradition, druids were able to pass on ancient teachings from generation to generation, often by way of poetry and verse. In this way many druids appear akin to the bards mentioned by other classical authors.

We know very little about Iron Age burials as few have been found, but a little more is known about religious beliefs. It was thought that the soul was indestructible and resided in the human head not the heart, hence the fascination with skulls and decapitation. People were said to believe in reincarnation and they worshipped a number of deities. Evidence for some of these deities has been found on Roman inscriptions around Northumberland, as the soldiers often incorporated the worship of local deities into their own religious duties. In Northumberland these local deities are known to include the gods Cocidius and Antenociticus, and the goddess Coventina. Sacrifices of both animals and humans were common and the druids were known for using the entrails of their enemies for divination.

Although little of the textual evidence of classical times can be related directly to Northumberland we should not forget the importance of the recent discoveries at the Roman fort at Vindolanda. The writing tablets recovered from the fort's waterlogged deposits have provided an unusually direct snapshot of daily life on this site. It is certainly possible that as more of these written sources come to light, and analysis proceeds, references to the indigenous British population will come to light. And it is with such hopes in mind that we can look forward to future discoveries around Northumberland.

Further Reading

General

Champion, T. C. and J. R. Collis, Eds. 1996. *The Iron Age in Britain and Ireland*. Sheffield: J.R. Collis.

Cunliffe, B. 1991. *Iron Age Communities in Britain*. London and New York 3rd edtn: Routledge.

Cunliffe, B. 1995. *Iron Age Britain*. London: B.T. Batsford/English Heritage.

Green, M. J. 1997. *Exploring the World of the Druids*. London: Thames and Hudson Ltd.

James, S. and V. Rigby (1997). *Britain and the Celtic Iron Age*. London, British Museum Press.

van der Veen, M. 1992. *Crop Husbandry regimes: An Archaeobotanical Study of Farming in Northern England, 1000 B.C. - A.D. 500*. Sheffield: Sheffield Archaeological Monograph 3.

Northumberland

Burgess, C. 1970. Excavations at the scooped settlement Hetha Burn I, Hethpool, Northumberland. *Transactions of the Architectural and Archaeological Society of Durham and Northumberland* 2: 1-26.

Burgess, C. 1984. The Prehistoric Settlement of Northumberland: A Speculative Survey. In R. Miket and C. Burgess (eds.) *Between And Beyond The Walls: Essays on the Prehistory and History of North Britain in Honour of George Jobey*. Edinburgh: John Donald: 126-175.

Charlton, B. and J. Day. 1978. Excavation and field survey in Upper Redesdale. *Archaeologia Aeliana* 5th series 6: 61-86.

Halliday, S. R. 1982. Later prehistoric farming in south-east Scotland. In D. W. Harding (ed.) *Later Prehistoric Settlement in in South-east Scotland*. Edinburgh: Edinburgh University Press. Department of Archaeology Occasional Paper 8: 75-91.

Hodgson, N., G. C. Stobbs, and M. van der Veen. 2001. An Iron Age Settlement and Remains of Earlier Prehistoric Date beneath South Shields Roman Fort, Tyne and Wear. *Archaeological Journal* 158: 62-160.

Jobey, G. 1964. Enclosed stone built settlements in North Northumberland. *Archaelogia Aeliana* 4th ser, 42: 41-64.

Jobey, G. 1965. Hillforts and Settlements in Northumberland. *Archaeologia Aeliana* 4th ser, 43: 21-64.

Jobey, G. 1971. Excavations at Brough Law and Ingram Hill. *Archaeologia Aeliana* 4th ser, 49: 71-93.

Jobey, G. 1973. A Romano-British settlement at Tower Knowe, Wellhaugh, Northumberland, 1972. *Archaeologia Aeliana* 5th ser, 1: 55-79.

Jobey, G. 1977. Iron Age and later farmsteads on Belling Law, Northumberland. *Archaeologia Aeliana* 5th ser, 5: 1-38.

Jobey, G. 1983. A note on some northern palisaded settlements. In A. O'Conner and D. V. Clarke (eds.) *From the Stone Age to the 'Forty Five*. Edinburgh: 197-205.

Jobey, G. and Tait, J. 1966. Excavations on palisaded settlements and cairnfields at Alnham, Northumberland. *Archaeologia Aeliana* 4th Ser. 44: 5-48.

McOmish, D. 1999. Wether Hill and Cheviots Hillforts. *Northern Archaeology* 17/18: 113-127.

Topping, P. 1981. The prehistoric field systems of College Valley: north Northumberland. *Northern Archaeology* 2(1): 14-33.

Topping, P. 1983. Observations on the stratigraphy of early agricultural remains in the Kirknewton area of the Northumberland Cheviots. *Northern Archaeology* 4(1): 21-31.

Topping, P. 1989. Early cultivation in Northumberland and The Borders. *Proceedings of the Prehistoric Society* 55: 161-179.

Topping, P. 1993. The excavation of an unenclosed settlement, field system and cord rig cultivation at Linhope Burn, Northumberland, 1989. *Northern Archaeology* 11: 1-42.

Topping, P. 1993. Lordenshaws Hillfort and its Environs. *Archaeologia Aeliana* 5th ser. 21: 15-27.

Waddington, C., K. Blood and J. Crow. 1998. Survey and Excavation at Harehaugh Hillfort and Possible Neolithic Enclosure. *Northern Archaeology* 15/16: 87-108.

Young, R. and T. Simmonds 1995. Marginality and the nature of later prehistoric upland settlement in the north of England. *Landscape History* 17: 5-16.

8 Places to Visit

Museums with Prehistoric Collections

Museum of Antiquities of Newcastle-upon-Tyne

This is the principal museum for the north-east region and contains a very fine collection of prehistoric material ranging from stone tools and pottery, to metalwork and cup-and-ring-marked rocks. It is open year-round from 10:00am until 5:00pm except Sundays. It is located in the Quadrangle next to the arches on the University of Newcastle campus. Admission free. Tel. 0191 2227846. Web Address http://museums.ncl.ac.uk/

Alnwick Castle Museum

This is a small but excellent museum located in the Postern Tower inside Alnwick Castle. It contains a wealth of prehistoric artefacts, including some particularly fine metalwork, set in a lively and colourful display. It is open from April to October with access between 11:00am and 5:00pm. Access to the museum is included in the admission charge to the castle. Tel. 01665 510777. Web Address http://www.alnwickcastle.com/

Visitor Centres with Prehistory Displays

Brigantium Archaeological Centre

The Brigantium Archaeological Centre differs from a typical museum as it seeks to tell the story of prehistoric Northumberland through a series of 'reconstructed' monuments from different periods. All the reconstructions are based on the excavated evidence from real sites in the valley that would otherwise not be able to be visited by the public as most are on private land. The centrepiece of the site is a magnificent stone-built roundhouse set inside an enclosure, as well as other monuments, an indoor display, video and shop. The site is located in Rochester village on the A697 in Redesdale (north of Otterburn) and is open from March to the end of October between 9:00am and 5:00pm. Tel. 01830 520801. Web Address http://museums.ncl.ac.uk/archive/

Maelmin Heritage Trail

The Maelmin Heritage Trail is an open-air site containing a short walk, partly in woodland, that describes the archaeology of the region from the arrival of the first humans through to the early medieval period. This is achieved through a sequence of information panels and two reconstructions; one of a Mesolithic hut and one of a late Neolithic henge. There is also a small nature trail on the site. Maelmin is located immediately off the A697 at the south end of Milfield village. The site is open all day, year-round, and admission is free. A guidebook, additional information and a display can be found in the village café. A schools pack has been produced for the site and enquiries should be sent to the author (CW) at the School of Historical Studies, University of Newcastle, NE1 7RU.

Northumberland National Park Visitor Centres: Ingram and Rothbury

The Northumberland National Park has impressive displays at a number of its visitor centres that provide information on the archaeological heritage of Northumberland. The Ingram centre has a display focusing on the archaeology of the Breamish valley, while the Rothbury centre has an audio-visual display and information boards. Both are open from March to November between 10:00am and 5:00pm and admission is free. These centres also stock a wide range of leaflets for archaeological sites to visit. The National Park produces its own range of self-guide leaflets to various archaeological sites (see also the 'Sites to Visit' section below).
Tel. Ingram 01665 578248, Rothbury 01669 620887.
Web Address: http://www.northumberland-national-park.org.uk

Wooler Tourist Information Centre

The Cheviot Centre in Wooler provides accommodation for the Tourist Information Centre and is home to an interactive archaeological display, while an example of heather thatch for a roundhouse roof can also be seen. Archaeological leaflets are also available here and it makes a good starting point for an expedition into the hills. It is open from March to the end of October between 10:00am and 5:00pm. Tel. 01668 282123. Web Address http://www.berwickonline.org.uk/guide/tic_wooler.htm

Sites to Visit

Broomridge, Goatscrag and Roughtin Lynn NT975370

Located to the east of Ford village this area of moorland is home to cup-and-ring-marked rocks, cairns and the site of a Mesolithic rock shelter at the base of Goatscrag. The largest cup-and-ring-marked rock in England is at Roughtin Lynn, in woodland at the east end of the moor. This site also has an impressive enclosure located next to it, consisting of three rows of banks and ditches. On the north side of Broomridge is the Ford Moss nature reserve where the industrial archaeological remains of an old coal mine can be seen.

Doddington Moor NT005318

This fascinating area of moorland on the east side of the Milfield basin contains some excellent archaeological remains and commands wonderful views across the Milfield plain towards the Cheviot Hills. An information board is located in the golf club car park that indicates the location of sites. The moor has some fine examples of cup-and-ring-marked rocks, together with a very impressive Iron Age hillfort at the far end of the golf course with the remains of internal roundhouses clearly visible. Elsewhere on the moor are other hillforts and enclosures as well as the remains of an unusual small stone circle, and cairns. The moor is most easily accessed by taking the road signposted to 'Wooler Golf Club' from Doddington village.

Harehaugh Hillfort NY970998

This well-preserved hillfort occupies a strategic position on a spur where the Coquet valley forks. The defences are quite complex and include a mixture of single, double and triple ramparts. Excavations have shown that the ramparts were stone-faced with a stout timber breastwork along the top. There is also evidence that an earlier, Neolithic, enclosure occupied this hilltop prior to the construction of the Iron Age fort. Traces of this can be seen running across the site once you have passed through the main entrance into the fort.

Howick NU259166
The Mesolithic and Bronze Age sites at Howick lie immediately next to the coastal path that runs along the cliff. Although there is nothing to see on the ground information panels have been installed at Craster TIC. This is a beautiful area to walk, with the Howick Burn lying immediately to the south of the site. A fully illustrated free archaeological leaflet can be picked up from Craster Tourist Information Centre where there are additional display boards explaining the archaeology of the Howick area.

Humbleton Hill Hillfort NT967283
This large stone-built fort commands a strong position overlooking Wooler and the Milfield basin. This Iron Age citadel has the remains of hut circles and scooped hut stances still visible inside it. Although the stone walls have largely tumbled down over the years there are still some examples of faced wall *in situ*. This hill was also the site of a battle between the English and Scots in 1402, and is remembered in the opening scenes of Shakespeare's 'Henry IV Part 1'. The National Park has produced a free self-guide leaflet to the site.

Breamish Valley NU019163
The Breamish valley is home to the picturesque village of Ingram and a National Park Visitor Centre where displays and leaflets about the surrounding archaeology can be picked up. There is a superb walk that takes the visitor over Bronze Age cultivation terraces to the Iron Age hillfort at Brough Law, where great views can be had from its stone ramparts. From here the walk takes you to two early Bronze Age cairns that have been fully excavated in recent years and on to the hillforts at Middle Dean and Wether Hill, before returning to Ingram village. You also pass a number of impressive cropmark sites on the way that have been excavated as part of a National Park project, with information about these available in the centre and in the various leaflets.

Old Bewick and Blawearie NU075216
The prominent high point on the sandstone escarpment occupied by Old Bewick hillfort commands an expansive view towards the Cheviots and is one of the most atmospheric places in the county. Perched on the crest of the escarpment, this large hillfort has multiple rings of defences consisting of banks and ditches, the former probably covering stone-faced ramparts. It is unusual in having a dividing set of ramparts between each half of the hillfort. The entrances can still be seen, together with two WWII pill boxes. To the east of the fort are some excellent cup-and-ring-marked rocks, while a number of robbed cairns can be seen to the west. To the north-east of the fort, near the track across the moor, are the well-preserved remains of the excavated ring cairn at Blawearie with its large kerbstones and cist graves. Further east still

is another small hillfort perched above the precipitous gorge of the Harehope Burn. This area of moor makes a superb walk that can be strenuous in places.

The Three Kings Stone Circle NT774001

This site is the remains of a type of stone circle known as a 'four-poster' and dates to the early Bronze Age. Although there are only three stones visible, excavations have shown that the site did indeed have four posts set in a rectangle with a low cairn inside. An information board is located on the site and further information about the monument can be found at nearby Brigantium. This delightful site is located on a woodland walk signposted from the Forest Enterprise car park at the start of the Forest Drive near Byreness. It is open all year round and access is free. It is most easily reached by using the signposted turning off the A68 trunk road, although during winter this road can be difficult to access.

Yeavering Bell Hillfort NT928293

Yeavering Bell is the largest hillfort in Northumberland and occupies the twin peaks of the most prominent of the northern chain of Cheviot Hills. The fort lies above the entrance to the Glen valley and commands extensive views across the Milfield basin. The walls survive as tumbled stone ramparts with annexes to the east and west. The entrances can still be seen, together with the platforms for dozens of roundhouses. The site can be reached by a footpath that leads from Old Yeavering off the B6351 road. A National Park self-guide leaflet has been produced for this site and can be obtained locally or at the National Park centres or information points.